THE ELEMENTS OF ALCHEMY

Cherry Gilchrist, a graduate of Cambridge University, is well-known as an author and a singer who specializes in baroque and early music. She has written many books and articles on alchemy, astrology, mythology and social history, and has worked in various capacities in publishing books on these subjects. She lectures widely and gives workshops centred on these themes.

The *Elements Of* is a series designed to present high quality introductions to a broad range of essential subjects.

The books are commissioned specifically from experts in their fields. They provide readable and often unique views of the various topics covered, and are therefore of interest both to those who have some knowledge of the subject, as well as those who are approaching it for the first time.

Many of these concise yet comprehensive books have practical suggestions and exercises which allow personal experience as well as theoretical understanding, and offer a valuable source of information on many important themes.

In the same series

THE ELEMENTS OF
ALCHEMY

Cherry Gilchrist

ELEMENT BOOKS

© Cherry Gilchrist 1991

Published in Great Britain in 1991 by
Element Books Limited
Longmead, Shaftesbury, Dorset

Published in the U.S.A. in 1991 by
Element Inc
42 Broadway, Rockport, MA 01966

Cover illustration: Images Colour Library
Cover design by Max Fairbrother
Typeset by Selectmove Ltd, London
Printed and bound in Great Britain
by Billings Ltd, Hylton Road, Worcester

British Library Cataloguing in Publication Data
Gilchrist, Cherry
The elements of alchemy.
1. Alchemy
I. Title
540.112

ISBN 1–85230–205–4

CONTENTS

PREFACE

When I was first asked to write on the subject of alchemy, about seven years ago, I agreed to do so with a carefree spirit. Little did I realise what complexities awaited me. My grounding in subjects such as the Cabbala, astrology, Christian mysticism and mythology was a solid one; I had actively and practically studied in this field for quite some time, and assumed that my brief excursions into alchemical literature could be padded out with no trouble at all.

This was not to be. I was both dazed and amazed by the profusion of alchemical texts, the discrepancies between them, the cryptic nature of their utterances, and the fact that no two writers on the history of alchemy ever agreed with one other. I soon came to a decision that, since I did not have a lifetime to complete the project, I would have to formulate my own way of working. This meant choosing texts of quality, according to a sense of their individual worth, and picking a new path through the jungle of alchemical history. In other words, contact with alchemy throws you back upon your own resources. So it has always been; the alchemical seeker had to work out his or her own solution to the riddles posed by the quest for gold. Like the aspiring alchemist, I was able to make use of available studies on the subject, but, ultimately, had to draw my own conclusions.

The main intention of this current book is to clarify the aims and history of alchemy, and to relate it both to other spiritual and esoteric practices, and to the arts and sciences that it influenced. In the latter category, new discoveries are frequently being made, and it is exciting to see how the symbolism and language of alchemy has affected mainstream culture. My own explorations into the links between alchemy and Baroque music form one chapter, and I have been pleased to draw upon the researches of authors like Charles Nicholl, who relates alchemy to theatre, elsewhere.

My early optimism that I would penetrate to the heart of alchemy with no problem was perhaps founded on a strong sense, which is still with me, that alchemy is in our life blood. Somehow its powerful symbolism holds a place in the collective psyche; its images occur in the dreams and fancies of people who have never read an alchemical text. In my own case, I had had experiences of dreams and spontaneous 'visions', which were revelations of the alchemical process, at a time when my own formal acquaintance with alchemy was very slight; various people have related similar experiences to me. (The great psychologist, C.G. Jung, found the same phenomenon, which intensified his interest in alchemy as a means of psychic transmission of archetypes.) As a child, I took great delight in making an 'Aladdin's Cave' (as I thought of it) in our coal fire, a glowing cavern into which I tossed little scraps of every different kind of burnable substance I could find, making a kind of fiery garden full of different coloured little flames. Unfortunately such early experiments in aesthetic alchemy were soon banned by my parents.

To my mind, alchemy is not just some quaint but outdated practice, only of historical interest. The terms by which we know it, as a tradition of lengthy laboratory work, may no longer apply, but the inner life, the dynamic process of alchemy delineated by image and symbol, can still be tapped to enliven and illuminate a number of both spiritual and practical enterprises – meditation, holistic healing, music, psychology and art, to name but a few. A study of alchemy opens up possibilities; the spirit of it still resides in human consciousness, and when we become acquainted with its language again, we can use it in our creative endeavours.

Bristol, May 1990

1 · WHAT IS ALCHEMY?

Alchemy is the art of transformation. The work of the alchemist is to bring about succeeding changes in the material he operates on, transforming it from a gross, unrefined state to a perfect and purified form. To turn base metals into gold is the simplest expression of this aim, and at the physical level this involves chemical operations performed with laboratory equipment. However, this is only one dimension of alchemy, since the 'base material' worked upon and the 'gold' produced may also be understood as man himself in his quest to perfect his own nature. Mainstream alchemy is a discipline involving physical, psychological and spiritual work, and if any one of these elements is taken out of context and said to represent the alchemical tradition, then the wholeness and true quality of alchemy is lost.

For several reasons, it is not an easy tradition to understand. Firstly, the chief medium of alchemical expression is through the use of mythological symbols, which are the perfect means of conveying information that can be interpreted at both a material and a spiritual level, but which defy a single and precise definition.

Secondly, alchemy's claims to produce extraordinary results in the physical world are hard to assess objectively. By the laws of science as normally understood today, it is not possible to convert other metals into gold,

1

except by nuclear fission. But since alchemy encompasses mental as well as physical participation it inevitably goes beyond the realms of material science in its scope and may be able to produce effects on the physical level that cannot be accounted for by normal chemistry. Additionally, as we shall see, the gold produced is usually said to be quite different from ordinary gold.

Thirdly, alchemy has a history stretching back for at least two thousand years and has been practised in Eastern, Arabic and Western societies. It would be surprising indeed if it showed a uniform tradition of practice. Like any study, it has attracted many types of people with widely differing motivations. There have always been alchemists who were out-and-out materialists, greedy to try and make themselves rich by mastering the secret of creating gold. Some were merely gullible, others fraudulent, performing fake transmutations and getting their gold from the pockets of their spectators and prospective pupils rather than through any success in the laboratory. Even among the sincere and dedicated alchemists, the emphasis of approach could be very different. Some were interested more in the chemical techniques of alchemy, others in the philosophical aspects. Some saw alchemy as a path to the true meaning of Christianity, while others saw in it possibilities for producing subtle and potent medicines.

The knowledge and aim that each practitioner brought to alchemy coloured his attitude to it, and to some extent defined his mode of operation. There are certain key symbols and processes in alchemy, but no two descriptions of it are identical, which has caused many a headache for those who try and trace its history and significance. Writers on alchemy, like the alchemists themselves, define the tradition from their own viewpoint and inclinations. This is inevitable: there is no such thing as an 'objective' interpretation of alchemy. This should not pose a problem provided that the reader realises that a scientific, psychological or spiritual training will undoubtedly create a different emphasis in a study of alchemy, since alchemy contains all these dimensions. Few of us are likely to be equally skilled and knowledgeable on all three levels, and our personal expertise and preference will determine our approach to alchemy and our insights into its operation. Taken at its most simple level, this means that a scientist will find alchemy of interest as a form of early chemistry, the psychologist will see it as a way of mapping the human psyche through symbolic descriptions, and the mystic will interpret it as a quest for divine knowledge.

Alchemy demands to be taken seriously; it has been practised by men of distinction in the fields of philosophy, science, medicine and divinity who were inspired by its aims and who dedicated much time and material resources to its pursuit. In this book I have attempted to give the tradition the respect that I feel is due to it, but at the same time to highlight some of the problems of interpretation, inviting the reader to consider their implications rather than offering simple solutions that would not do justice to the questions raised.

THE NAME ALCHEMY

The immediate derivation of the word alchemy is from the Arabic *al kimia*. *Al* means 'the', but the meaning of the second half of the word is not at all clear. One popular idea is that it is associated with the Egyptian word *chem*, signifying 'black' and relating to the description of Egypt as 'The Land of the Black Soil'. This would then define alchemy as 'The Egyptian Art' or 'The Black Art'. Some scholars, though, consider it more likely that the word is derived from *chyma*, a Greek word relating to the casting or fusing of metal. This in turn appears to come from *cheein*, meaning 'to pour out'; *cheein* has other variants, such as *chymos*, 'plant juice', and *chylos*, a similar word but with the added association of 'taste'. It is possible that in the early days of alchemy the working of metals and the extraction of juices from plants were closely linked. (Readers who would like to investigate the etymology further are advised to read Chapter 4 of *The Origins of Alchemy in Graeco-Roman Egypt* by Jack Lindsay, which is entirely devoted to this topic.)

THE TIME-SPAN OF ALCHEMY

The origins of alchemy cannot be precisely dated, but it emerged as an art in its own right during the last two or three centuries BC, both in the Far East (especially in China), and in Western civilization. In the West it centred on the Alexandrian culture, drawing together aspects of both the Egyptian and the classical Greek worlds. The alchemy of the East had a preoccupation with creating an elixir of longevity, while that of the Graeco-Egyptian culture dealt chiefly with metals and minerals. Both aspired to knowledge of creation and universal order; both schools fell into a decline by the fifth and sixth centuries AD. However, while the Eastern tradition carried on (with cyclical ups and downs) right through the succeeding centuries, the Western school shifted location into the Arabic world, where it was enthusiastically practised and developed until Europeans climbed back out of the 'Dark Ages' and began to take an interest in the traditions of learning that the Arabs had preserved. From the twelfth century onwards, most European countries adopted alchemy as a study in its own right. Its reputation fluctuated. Sometimes it was considered to be a most elevated study, worthy to be practised by royalty, while sometimes it was looked upon as the profession of rogues and knaves.

During the sixteenth and seventeenth centuries there was an eagerness among men of learning to gather the strands of study together, to compare and synthesise the arts, sciences, and systems of occult and divine knowledge. Triggered by the Renaissance ideal, and perpetuated by such bodies as the Rosicrucian school of philosophy, this movement gained momentum and resulted in alchemy being brought out more into the open and set alongside other disciplines. Until then, it had been treated as a secret, private study, whose knowledge was only to be passed on directly by word of mouth or through the ambiguity of symbol and allegory. As it was discussed and practised more freely, so its quality changed. Many of the principles, symbols and ideas of alchemy were incorporated into the other branches of learning, such as medicine, music and literature;

4

alchemy itself receded from the public eye and was indeed thought extinct by many.

However, until the present day it has been practised quietly by a few adherents, and the tradition is now arousing new interest. Its imagery has shown its enduring value by finding a place in modern psychology, and the practice of a discipline that involves both scientific and psychic skills is again showing its appeal. Alchemy has reached a point of reappraisal and, re-formulated, it may once again be considered a serious subject for study.

THE AIM OF ALCHEMY

Alchemists have always looked upon their work as a way of life, insisting that it needs dedication and sincerity of intention if it is to produce any results. They speak of it in such terms as 'our sacred philosophy', the 'work of wisdom', the 'Great Work', and the 'divine activity'. The term 'our' is used freely in alchemical texts ('our gold', 'our mercury', 'our work', etc), implying, not possessiveness, but a special alchemical form of substances and secret methods of preparation that were understood only by the true practitioners and not by outsiders. It was a way of distinguishing alchemy from ordinary pharmacy and metal-working, but it also had the effect of suggesting the existence of an exclusive band of initiates who had access to knowledge denied to ordinary mortals. While this made it clear that alchemy was more than a material craft, such secrecy also helped to induce the envy and ridicule that has dogged alchemists throughout the centuries.

The fundamental aim of alchemy was the production of the *Philosopher's Stone*, also known as the *Elixir*, or *Tincture*. The proof of the Stone was that it would turn a base metal into gold. Thus the transmutation into gold was seen as a mark of success, but the power lay in the Stone itself, which was the transmuting agent. It is easy for these two elements to become confused in the interpretation of alchemy, and even the alchemical texts themselves are not always clear on this point. The

Stone is usually said to have something of the nature of gold in itself; it is the active element that was thought to accelerate the natural process of perfection in material. (Gold, as we shall see, was said to grow from base metals within the earth, and alchemical transmutation was therefore a speeded-up process of evolution.) The gold it could produce, however, was frequently said to be quite different from ordinary gold, being a more perfect form, and was accordingly called by such terms as 'our gold', 'exalted gold' or 'the gold of the Sages'.

The Stone was not usually described as stone-like in substance, but more often referred to as a powder or wax that could also be rendered into a liquid form, which corresponds better with its other appellations of Tincture or Elixir. Its power was not only as an agent of metallic transformation, but as the very secret of transformation itself, both in the physical and the spiritual realms:

> The Philosopher's Stone is called the most ancient, secret or unknown, natural incomprehensible, heavenly, blessed sacred Stone of the Sages. It is described as being true, more certain than certainty itself, the arcanum of all arcana – the Divine virtue and efficacy, which is hidden from the foolish, the aim and end of all things under heaven, the wonderful epilogue of conclusion of all the labours of the Sages – the perfect essence of all the elements, the indestructible body which no element can injure, the quintessence; the double and living mercury which has in itself the heavenly spirit – the cure for all unsound and imperfect metals – the everlasting light – the panacea for all diseases – the glorious Phoenix – the most precious of all treasures – the chief good of Nature.[1]

The Stone was seen as the key to knowledge, which only a wise man can use responsibly:

> If an athlete know not the use of his sword, he might as well be without it; and if another warrior that is skilled in the use of that weapon come against him, the first is likely to fare badly. For he that has knowledge and experience on his side, must carry off the victory.
>
> In the same way, he that possesses this tincture, by the grace of Almighty God, and is unacquainted with

its uses, might as well not have it all ... [But] whoever uses this as a medium shall find whither the vestibules of the palace lead, and there is nothing comparable to the subtlety thereof. He shall possess all in all, performing all things whatsoever which are possible under the sun.[2]

It was made very plain that alchemy was just as much to do with self-mastery as with mastery of the physical laws of Nature, and that neither could be achieved without patience, observation and devotion. Sometimes the aspect of personal transformation was stated very clearly; John of Rupescisia wrote in the fourteenth century that alchemy is 'the secret of the mastery of fixing the sun in our own sky, so that it shines therein and sheds light and the principle of light upon our bodies'.

THE ALCHEMICAL PROCESS

The art of the alchemist, then, is to activate a process that will transform a first substance, or prima materia, into the Philosopher's Stone. The process is of tremendous importance and carries no guarantee of success, since the attitude of the alchemist, the timing of events, and the type of materials and equipment used, must all harmonise and combine in exactly the right way. Often alchemists spent several decades in their search and attributed their ultimate success to outside aid – either divine or human – rather than to variation in their technique. After looking through various alchemical texts one is left with the impression that there was in fact no one precise formula, which, if followed to the letter, would bring about the desired end. There are only principles of operation that the alchemist must apply with a high level of awareness and judgement. Indeed, the process, with all its potential set-backs and problems, is itself the education of the alchemist, and until he has developed his own skills and insights through this he cannot perfect the Work.

The alchemist is described as the artist who, through his operations, brings Nature to perfection. But the process is also like the unfolding of the Creation of the world, to which the alchemist is a witness as he watches the changes that take place within the vessel. The vessel is a universe in miniature, a crystalline sphere through which he is privileged to see original drama of transformation:

> Neither be anxious to ask whether I actually possess this precious treasure. Ask rather whether I have seen how the world was created; whether I am acquainted with the nature of the Egyptian darkness, what is the cause of the rainbow; what will be the appearance of the glorified bodies at the general resurrection . . .[3]

The process itself consists of taking the primal material and subjecting it to chemical treatment, chiefly by heat and distillation, until it finally – perhaps only after years – comes to perfection. The body, soul and spirit of the matter, known as salt, mercury and sulphur, must be freed from their primitive state and reconcile in a new harmony. In terms of physical operation, alchemy differs from chemistry in its insistence on two factors: firstly, the timing of operations to accord with appropriate astrological configurations; and secondly, the repetition of certain stages of the process to an extraordinary extent (such as distilling a liquid several hundred times). Some writers on alchemy, emphasising its value as a spiritual discipline, have belittled the importance of its physical operations, but there is no doubt that the processing of physical substances was equally important in the art. Archibald Cockren, a twentieth-century alchemist, explains the necessity of this:

> That this preparation is a physical process carried out in a laboratory with water, retorts, sand-bath, and furnaces, there is no doubt. That alchemy is purely a psychic and spiritual science has no basis in fact. A science to be a science must be capable of manifestation on every plane of consciousness; in other words it must be capable of demonstrating the axiom 'as above, so below'. Alchemy can withstand this test, for it is, physically, spiritually, and psychically, a science manifesting throughout all form and all life.[4]

As I have implied, one can only talk about the different stages of the process in general terms, since descrip-

Fig. 1 *The double-headed dragon, containing sun and
moon, male and female within it.*

tions of it vary. Most texts also indicate that they are
holding back a particular secret, which is essential for
the completion of the operation. Often this relates to
the primal material, the substance needed to start the
process, whose composition is only hinted at. We will
look at this fascinating mystery later, but for the moment
it is enough to say that the first material of alchemy is
frequently described as something of metallic origin,
yet not outwardly resembling a metal, a base substance
known to all yet recognised only by the wise. The outward form of the primal material must be destroyed,
by fire or special acidic preparations. Sometimes this
is described as setting the two dragons at war with
one another. Thus the male and female principles of
the matter are released and can be reunited in a stage
often depicted as the marriage of the King and Queen.
Through initial conflict and division energy becomes
available, a source of fuel for the entire operation. Further treatment of the substance in the vessel by heat
leads to its 'death', a moment known as the *nigredo*,
or 'blackening'. But the 'soul' of the matter still lingers
in the hermetically sealed vessel, and may be induced
to condense in liquid form and return to the body once
more. This is the resurrection, which may be heralded
by a glorious show of irridescent colours known as 'The

9

Peacock's Tail'. The child of the royal union must be gently nurtured, usually by adding a liquid that may have been extracted from the vessel at an earlier stage. With the right food and heat it grows until it 'whitens', indicating that the Elixir is perfected in its first degree. The White Stone, as it is known, is said to be capable of transmuting metals into silver. It is the female tincture, equated with the moon. To gain the gold-giving tincture, the sun, further treatment is necessary until the Elixir reddens. Then it is the Red Rose, grown from the White Rose, the ultimate goal of the process.

As can be seen, alchemy describes its operations in vividly symbolic statements. Terms such as birth, death and resurrection are not used as mere associations but as indications of real states through which the matter and the soul of the alchemist must pass. The use of beasts, birds and archetypal human figures who fight, marry and copulate expresses the dynamic energies of the process. The different colours of each stage are the heraldic colours of transformation, announcing the dawning of a new 'day' in the creation.

2 · THE SEARCH FOR TRANSFORMATION

Gold is the focal symbol of alchemy. It is the crowning glory of the Work, the most perfect of metals, and every alchemist has aimed to master the secret of its creation. Gold is more than a metal – it is a principle; and thus, while physical, metallic gold holds a central position in alchemy, yet we also meet with the ideas of exalted gold, vegetable gold, and spiritual gold.

When we look at the properties of gold, it becomes apparent that it is a very special metal. It is almost immune to the normal processes of decay; it does not rust or tarnish. Fire will refine gold but not destroy it or change its basic nature. Aesthetically it has been described as having 'a smooth, soft texture, a beauty of colour, and a capacity to shine steadily'.[1] For the metal worker, it has considerable attractions since it can, if necessary, be worked cold. It is soft, which means that though it cannot be used for making sharp or durable implements, it can be crafted into delicately tooled shapes and patterns; it can also be beaten to an incredible thinness to form gold foil or leaf.

Gold is found in all the continents of the earth and has therefore been known to every human civilisation. The first known examples of gold worked by man appear around the fourth millenium BC. In Egypt and Ur, gold was used for jewellery, vessels, ornaments, and the adornment of royal tombs; it was not used as currency, however, until about 400 BC. In Egypt gold production was a state-controlled operation and accounts of conditions in the mines paint a gruesome picture of forced labour by criminals and prisoners of war.

From early times, gold was associated with royalty and divinity. The Egyptians called gold 'the flesh of the gods', and, along with other ancient peoples, saw attributes of divinity within gold – effulgence, purity, incorruptibility. Thus gold itself embodied the power of the divine, and could confer especial blessings and gifts through its use. Golden vessels, for instance, were thought to transform the quality of the drink they contained.

Gold also had an early correspondence with the sun, which the alchemists maintained, naming gold and silver as sun and moon, king and queen, the heavenly pair. Gold has also been esteemed universally as a magical, influential, other-worldly metal. In European traditions, fairies and dwarves were thought to be in possession of fabulous amounts of gold, and used it to tempt mortals into their kingdom. It was not merely a symbol of wealth, but an attribution of fairy land itself. There, the roof is made 'o' the beaten gould', the horses are shod with golden shoes, and the music comes from golden harps. Sometimes there is a golden bridge by which the spirits enter and leave their kingdom. Gold is associated with power, danger, enchantment and transformation. In nearly all cultures in which it is esteemed it has been valued as more than a mere metal, and it is this power of gold which the alchemists acknowledged and chose to represent as the goal of their work.

THE METAL WORKERS

The craft of metal work helped to build a foundation for alchemy, and had already been in existence long before alchemy itself first came to light around 200 BC. Alchemy was strongly influenced by Egyptian traditions, and Egypt had been a centre for metal workers who raised their craft to a high degree. They knew how to make alloys, and how to tint metals; they could colour gold with varnishes and understood gold plating. Some of their art was directed towards satisfying the ever-present human desire to obtain more for less, since there were recipes for debasing gold with other metals to increase its apparent weight, and even to make fake gold.

However, the craftsmen undoubtedly took a great pride in their work, and they guarded its secrets jealously. We have few details of how it was practised, but certain general principles are known from paintings or hieroglyphs of the time. The smelter's furnace, for instance, was built up high on three sides to intensify the heat when the metal was being refined, and a blowpipe was used to increase the height of the flames. The earliest alchemists would probably have been initiated into the art of metal work, but exactly how and when the two arts began to take on a separate identity is not certain.

THE FIRST ALCHEMISTS IN THE WEST

We only know of the existence of alchemists if they chose to reveal their presence, and if their writings have survived them. Therefore, while the earliest alchemical texts we now have date from the third century BC, according to some authorities, we cannot tell how many practising alchemists there were before this date, or how strong the tradition was at its recorded inception, since there are very few texts available until we come to the fourth to seventh centuries AD, the period that marks the first flowering of alchemy in the West. Although the alchemists themselves have always claimed a venerable pedigree for their art, stretching back to Plato, Moses and the god Hermes himself, this is no help in dating its origins.

These claims sprang from a philosophy which maintained that in the past man was the master of all wisdom, and that his passage through time has been marked by a gradual forgetting of the ancient secrets which only true initiates had kept uncorrupted throughout the centuries. It was common, therefore for authors to establish a worthy pedigree for their writings, by ascribing their teachings to earlier masters, or by claiming direct descent from the original divine or mythical patrons of the art. It was an attempt to lend weight to their words, rather than to deceive. Nevertheless, this does not help the historian, and we find that the beginnings of alchemy are shrouded in obscurity. The first known and named alchemical text is probably that by **Bolos of Mendes**, who wrote a book entitled *Physika*. This dealt with a variety of alchemical and pseudo-alchemical crafts, such as the making of gold, silver, gems, and the production of purple dye. Bolos tried to ascribe his work to the philosopher Demokrites (Democritus), father of the atomic theory, who lived in the fifth century BC. It is possible that the writings of Bolos date to around 250 BC, but some authorities would regard them as products of the first or second century AD. Other early extant texts are known as the Leiden and Stockholm Papyri, but these, while going under the name of alchemy, seem to be merely collections of recipes for making false gold and silver and for tinting and alloying metals. One recipe begins: 'To give objects of copper the appearance of gold so that neither the feel nor rubbing on the touchstone will discover it . . .'

With these texts we move to the early years of the current era, and to the flourishing Alexandrian culture in which alchemy throve. Alexandria was founded as a city by the Emperor Alexander on the north coast of Egypt in the fourth century BC and soon became a centre of great influence in the fields of philosophy, mathematics, astrology, science, medicine, and indeed every other branch of learning then practised. It was a city of mixed nationalities, containing Greek, Jewish, Egyptian, Persian, Syrian and Christian inhabitants. When powerful cultures meet in peace or war there is often a remarkable stimulation of ideas; the coming together of the European and Arabic cultures at the time of the Crusades can be cited as an example. In Alexandria this contact was affirmed and crystallized through the founding of schools of learning and the establishment of the great Alexandrian library. Scholars travelled from far and wide to study the ancient and contemporary texts housed there, which represented the whole spectrum of knowledge of the classical and Egyptian civilizations. Had this library not been destroyed at a later date by the Arab invasion, our knowledge of the ancient world would be infinitely greater than it is.

Another notable name from this early period of Alexandrian alchemy is that of **Maria the Jewess**, who is quoted with respect by other alchemists of the time and who lived around AD 100. She seems to have been a practical and inventive lady who improved the alchemical apparatus of the day. The *bain-marie* is named after her – the warm water bath that allows gentle cooking and that is still used in modern kitchens. Certain other texts from the same period are ascribed to **Kleopatra**, and while most historians are inclined to regard this as an attempt to elevate the famous Queen Cleopatra to the status of an alchemical priestess, Jack Lindsay, on the other hand, considers that the works originate from the school of a different Kleopatra, a lady alchemist of the time whose teachings were perpetuated by her disciples. The writings in question are *The Dialogue of Kleopatra and the Philosophers* and *The Gold-Making of Kleopatra*. From the former comes a precise description of the alchemical process:

> Take from the four elements the arsenic which is highest and lowest, the white and the red, the male and the female in equal balance, so that they may be joined to one another. For just as the bird warms her eggs with her heat and brings them to their appointed term, so yourselves warm your composition and bring it to its appointed term. And when you've borne it out and caused it to drink of the divine Waters in the Sun and in heated places, cook it upon a gentle fire with the virginal milk, keeping it from the smoke. Then shut the ingredients up in Hades and stir carefully until the preparation becomes thicker and does not run from the fire. Then remove it from the fire; and when the soul and spirit are unified and become one, project upon the body of silver and you will have gold such as the treasuries of kings do not contain.[2]

One of the best known authors of the period is **Zosimos**, whose writings give us some fine examples of visionary alchemy which will be considered in the next chapter.

Laboratory work was certainly prominent in early alchemy, and a good deal of information survives as to the type of equipment used. *Cupellation*, a technique already known in ancient Egypt, was used to refine metals. A cupel consisted of a crucible, made usually of bone ash, which was supported by its lips about the edge of a furnace. The metal to be refined was placed within it and it was subjected to intense heat, sometimes closed in a kiln for several days until the impurities were either driven off by the heat or absorbed into the crucible itself.

A special feature of alchemy was *distillation*, and it remained a technique unique to alchemy for many centuries (see p. 103). A *still*, or *alembic* was used. The material to be heated would be placed at the bottom of the still; there was a cool section above to condense the vapour driven off by the heat, and some means of collecting the liquid thus distilled.

Another invention of the time was the *kerotakis*, a piece of equipment that created vapours out of a substance, through the application of heat; the vapours would then affect a portion of metal placed in the top part of the apparatus. The result would frequently emerge as an alloy, but it is likely that the idea of imparting colour through the use of the kerotakis was also important, since the word carries the meaning of 'artist's palette'.

From the earliest days, colour changes have played a significant part in alchemy. Each stage of the process has been associated with a different colour, and a correct sequence of colour changes has always been considered of critical importance in ascertaining whether the work is proceeding along the right lines. To the alchemists, colour has always been much more than an outward quality of matter; colour is the *pneuma* or life spirit of a substance. Changes of colour are a visible sign that transformation is taking place within matter.

The Greek alchemists recognised four distinct stages of colour change in the process, a successive blackening, whitening, yellowing and reddening of the material in the vessel. (Sometimes red and purple were used synonymously.) Black was equated with the death of matter, and white with its rebirth in a purified form. The exact meaning of the yellowing is not clear, and this stage was often omitted in later descriptions of alchemy; but the reddening was always seen as the final perfection of the matter that had been transformed from a gross state into the longed-for Stone or Tincture. Although it was considered that no stage had been successfully accomplished unless the appropriate colour was manifested, yet it should be noted that colour on its own did not necessarily denote success. Warning is given, for instance, of a premature reddening, which could occur through hasty and careless work and which must be corrected at once.

The key sequence of black, white and red has remained throughout the history of alchemy, with occasional variations and additions. The most common addition is that of the irridescent stage known as the *Peacock's Tail*, the rainbow, or the starry sky, which usually occurs after the *nigredo*, or blackening. Colour is an intrinsic part of the alchemical drama; with a little imagination the reader can easily see how, after perhaps months of patient observation, the alchemist was affected profoundly by the appearance of a new and dazzling hue in the hermetic vessel.

THEORIES OF ELEMENTS AND METALS

There are four elements, and ... each has at its center another element which makes it what it is. These are the four pillars of the world. They were in the beginning evolved and moulded out of chaos by the hand of the Creator; and it is their contrary action which keeps up the harmony and equilibrium of the mundane machinery; it is they, which through the virtue of celestial influences, produce all things above and beneath the earth.

Michael Sendivogius, writing in the seventeenth century, is here describing a classical theory of the construction of matter that formed the basis of ideas on alchemical transformation from the early period until the eighteenth century. The four elements are earth, water, fire and air, and were first mentioned by the Greek philosopher Empedocles, who flourished c.450 BC. These were seen as combining in different proportions to form every substance in existence; in alchemy part of the task was to rearrange the composition of the elements and their relationship to one another in order to transform the substance itself.

Aristotle's exposition of the theory was formulated c.350 BC and held sway in Europe until the new era of science dawned in the seventeenth century. He held that each element was composed of two qualities, there being four qualities in all – hot, dry, moist and cold. The element of air was hot and moist; fire was hot and dry; earth dry and cold; and water cold and moist. By changing a quality of each element, transformation became possible: by driving out the moisture from air, for instance, fire would result since the pair of qualities would now be those of fire, which was hot and dry. This provided the alchemists with a theory of transformation.

The apparent simplicity of this system, however, is undermined by the alchemists' own descriptions of it, as we can see from the quotation above. They were quick to point out that true air, fire, water and earth were not the common entities that we know. The 'common' elements were the visible or tangible qualities that came closest in character to the 'pure' elements. These pure elements were found only at the very heart of matter, and were seen more as forces, or agencies, rather than as detectable substances. They carried out the work of Nature by combining and recombining to create all the different types of matter on the earth. If matter changed its state, as it did in the alchemical vessel, then this signified that the proportions of elements forming the matter had been transformed and recombined. A change in the elemental state could not be brought about by mere physical force, such as by grinding or cutting. Usually it was though to be produced only by the application of another elemental agent, that of fire or water especially.

Thus 'common' fire and water played a prominent part in alchemy, but frequently the alchemists sought to make the 'pure' forms, which they called by such names as 'our fire' and 'the sweet water', the 'Pontic water' or 'the water of the wise'. These were the subject of lengthy preparation and were used for such purposes as the destruction of the original form of the Primal Material in order to liberate the elements within it, or for nourishing the material in the vessel when it had already undergone radical transformation.

Gold was considered to contain the perfect balance of all four elements. Nature, it was said, operated a constant process of perfecting that which was originally gross or corrupt. Aristotle, once again, was responsible for first putting forward the theory that Nature 'grew' gold in the earth and that all metals, in due course, would grow to become gold. Metals themselves grew from seeds, which might not normally be recognised as being metallic in their primal state. Sometimes the alchemical quest for the Primal Material was described as a search for the right metallic seed, which the alchemist could nurture and grow into its perfect golden state. Aristotle suggested that metals were produced within the earth by the action of vapour. Alchemists elaborated this idea, inferring that the warmth of the sun and the influence of the planets activate this vapour, and that because these factors vary according to the climate, the seasons, and the planetary configurations, so the types of metals laid down in the earth will vary. In the alchemical process they sought to imitate this, by taking the degree of heat in the furnace, the time of year, and the astrological indications into account. By observing Nature, the wise handmaid of the divine Will, the alchemist could begin to understand her ways, it was said, and learn how to imitate and improve on them through Art.

The alchemist's view of the earth was of a living organism that was in a constant state of change and growth. In alchemy there is no such thing as 'dead' matter; all substance has life and movement.

EASTERN ALCHEMY: THE SEARCH FOR THE ELIXIR

In many ways the development of alchemy in the Far East is remarkably similar to that of alchemy in the West, especially in the first thousand years of their existence. Scholars are not able to agree about the reasons for this. Some argue that alchemy began in the East and was transmitted by connections as yet untraced to the West, while some consider the reverse to be more likely. Others, such as H.J. Shepperd[3] argue for independent origins in East and West, with possible cross-fertilization at a later stage, such as a Chinese influence on Arabian alchemy in the seventh century AD. Shepperd points out that metallurgic skills developed independently in different cultures as a natural part of human evolution, and that these involved a secrecy and mystery that would have given rise to alchemical work almost spontaneously.

There are differences of emphasis in the Eastern and Western histories of alchemy, even though both sought the transformation of earthly materials into a divine potency. In the West the quest was primarily concerned with the transmutation of gold, whether for physical or spiritual purposes. In the East alchemists aspired to make a perfect elixir of gold which would bring immortality to the soul and supernatural powers to the mind, such as the ability to tap the knowledge of the celestial beings:

> My teacher also used to say that if one wished for perpetual life one should diligently take the great medicines, and that if one desired to communicate with the gods and spirits one should use solutions of metals and practise the multiplication of one's person. By multiplying the person one will be able automatically to see the three hun souls and the seven pho souls within one's body. One will also be able to enter the presence of the powers and principalities of the heavens, and the deities of the earth, as well as having the spirits of all the mountains and rivers in one's service.[4]

Gold was venerated in the East from ancient times. One of the Indian Veda, written around the eighth century BC, mentions the use of a golden talisman to prolong life, and from the seventh century BC comes the saying: 'Gold is indeed fire, light and immortality'. The first real records of alchemy date from the first few centuries AD, parallelling Western development. It is known that alchemy was practised in India, Tibet and Burma, but the best information available to us concerns China (due mainly to the researches of Joseph Needham).

Alchemy in China had its roots in Taoism, a branch of religious philosophy. In both alchemy and Taoism there seems to be an idea of a Spirit in all things that is greater than anything else in the world, and yet ignored by all:

> The great Tao flows everywhere, both to the left and to the
>   right.
> The ten thousand things depend upon it; it holds nothing
>   back.
> It fulfils its purpose silently and makes no claim.
>
> It nourishes the ten thousand things,
> And yet is not their lord.
> It has no aim; it is very small.
>
> The ten thousand things return to it,
> Yet it is not their lord.
> It is very great.
>
> It does not show greatness,
> And is therefore truly great.*

Alchemy in China absorbed other elements of the prevailing culture and philosophies. The school of the Naturalists (c.350–270 BC) promoted an interest in science and the discovery of the properties of matter. Five elements were said to compose the basis of the material world: they were called earth, wood, metal, fire and water. These did not have quite the same connotations as the classical Western elements, and appear to have defined qualities of plasticity and permeability. The element of wood, for instance, was said to represent that quality in matter which determines whether a surface is curved or straight; the element of metal was taken as the property of a substance that allows melting and moulding to take place.

Alchemy in the West used astrology as a guide to the correct timing of events; Chinese alchemy did the same, and added the use of the *I Ching*, the divinatory Book of Changes. Chinese alchemy did not restrict itself solely to the preparation of the Elixir, but also embodied a quest for transmutation of metals as a subsidiary interest. Huan

*Compare this with the description of the first material on p. 42

21

T'an, in the first century BC, was said to have had a drug that would convert quicksilver into gold. Neither were charlatans restricted to Western alchemy; we may infer their existence in China from an edict published around 144 BC commanding public execution of all those who were counterfeiting gold.

Laboratory experiment was an intrinsic part of Eastern alchemical practice. This led to the understanding of various chemical principles and by about the third century BC the Taoists had already grasped the technique of condensation. In the fourth century AD an emperor set up a Taoist laboratory to conduct alchemical experiments. This particular establishment had a rather curious aspect to it, however; condemned criminals were used as guinea pigs to test the elixirs that the industrious alchemists produced! One wonders whether this was a cruel and cowardly procedure, or a generous gesture to give the condemned men one last chance!

3 · DREAMS AND REVELATIONS

How did alchemists acquire their knowledge? There were teachers, manuscripts and, later, printed books from which they might learn. But accounts of alchemical discoveries frequently relate that the key to the mystery was found through a personal vision or revelation. It was also emphasised that such illumination could only come to those who were sincere, persistent, and well-prepared to receive the secret knowledge:

> A most wonderful Magistery and Archimagistery is the Tincture of sacred Alchemy, the marvellous science of the secret Philosophy, the singular gift bestowed upon men through the grace of Almighty God – which men have never discovered through the labour of their own hands, but only by revelation and the teaching of others.[1]

This idea of a direct revelation, frequently expressed through a vision or dream, clarifies many of the aspects of alchemy which at first seem bewildering. It sheds light on why alchemical descriptions are nearly always given in terms of verbal or pictorial symbols, and it helps us to understand why no one account of the alchemical process ever seems to follow exactly the same lines as another. Even allowing for the difference between individual schools of alchemy, the fact is that each alchemist demonstrates his art in an original way, just as no person's dream is ever exactly the same as another's.

The philosophy underlying this approach to alchemy, but by no means unique to it, is that *knowledge exists*, and that we can attune ourselves to receive it. It is possible for individual consciousness to link into a consciousness of a higher order and learn from it. Knowledge revealed in this way is unlikely to surface in a precise or literal form; it exists at the level of what we call archetypes, a level of principle and abstract understanding. It will thus be received more as the seed of an idea, something that can be developed, and given an external application. Moreover, a person will receive and understand an idea according to his own cultural background and the age in which he lives. Knowledge is like a pool; a man dips his pitcher into the pool and the water he carries away adapts itself to the form of this particular container.

Alchemy is not alone in transmitting a tradition of personal revelation as a means of penetrating the mysteries of the world. Many religions embody accounts of dreams, visions and encounters with divine messengers that bring wisdom and understanding, and it is generally accepted that the most profound religious understanding is likely to come through revelation and internal illumination. It is less commonly considered that knowledge can also arise in this way in relation to many other aspects of life. We have become used to the idea that 'facts' and 'theories' are built up only through a process of trial and error and planned experiment. Yet, it seems, this is far from the truth, even in science, as A.M. Taylor points out: 'The history of science shows us, again and again, great discoveries made by passionate adherence to ideas forged in the white heat of imagination.'[2] He also reminds us that some of the most important scientific ideas did *not* fit the facts as they could be demonstrated, and that the scientists concerned had to persist with their visions, despite the apparent evidence, until the data available could expand to demonstrate the truth of their theories.

But while the science of today may be shy of admitting the power of the Idea, and even more wary of ascribing its birth to the activity of a higher form of consciousness, alchemy had no such scruples and indeed the alchemists believed that their art could never be mechanical and would only be accomplished through access to a source of wisdom. (Even those who were taught by a living adept held, by and large, to the idea that 'the master will come when the pupil is ready'.) The chief medium of alchemical revelation, the way in which the 'Idea' surfaced into consciousness, was that of the vision. The *Corpus Hermeticum*, a body of hermetic writings originating from the early centuries of the Christian era (see p. 92) begins thus:

> Once upon a time, when I had begun to think about the things that are, and my thoughts had soared high aloft, while my bodily senses had been put under restraint by sleep – yet not such sleep as that of men weighed down by fullness of food or by bodily weariness – methought there came to me a Being of vast and boundless magnitude, who called me by name, and said to me, 'What do you wish to hear and see, and to learn and to come to know by thought?' 'Who are you?' I said. 'I,' said he, 'am Poimandres, the Mind of the Sovereignty.' 'I would feign learn,' said I, 'the things that are, and understand their nature, and get knowledge of God.'

The dreamer is then taught about the role of the elements of nature in the creation of the world.

One of the most famous visionary alchemical accounts was written by Zosimos and included in his work *On Virtue* (fourth century AD). He recounts that he fell asleep while reciting alchemical formulae to himself and:

> I saw a sacrificing priest who stood above me by an altar shaped like a chalice. The altar had fifteen steps leading up to it. The priest stood up, and I heard a loud voice from above which said to me, 'I have completed the act of descending the fifteen steps, walking into darkness, and the act of climbing the steps towards the light. It is the sacrificer who renews me by rejecting the denseness

of the body. Thus, consecrated a priest by necessity, I become a spirit.'

Having heard the voice of him who stood above on the chalice-shaped altar, I demanded to know who he was. And he, in a shrill voice replied thus: 'I am Ion, the priest of the sanctuaries, and I have undergone intolerable violence. Someone came suddenly in the morning and he took me by force, cleaving me in two with a sword, dismembering me, following the rules of combination. He took off all the skin from my head with the sword which he held, he mixed my bones with my flesh, and he burnt them in the fire of the process. It was thus that I learnt, through the transformation of the body, to become a spirit, so intolerable was the violence.' As I forced him to speak to me thus, his eyes became like blood and he vomited up all his flesh. And I saw him take the appearance of a tiny man, tearing himself with his own teeth and falling away.

Filled with fear, I woke up and I thought, 'Is this not the composition of the waters?' I told myself that I had understood this well, and I fell asleep again.

More visions follow, which Zosimos interprets as being teachings about the divine water, giving him a complete key to the process of alchemical transformation.

In a word, when all things are brought to agreement by division and union, without neglecting the process, nature is transformed; for nature, returning to herself, transforms herself, and this concerns the quality and the bond of virtue throughout the whole universe.

Zosimos then turns his whole vision into a symbolic description of the alchemical process to serve as a model for other seekers:

In brief, my friend, build a temple of one stone, resembling white lead, alabaster, with no beginning nor end in its construction. It should have within it a source of pure water, sparkling like the sun. Observe carefully on which side of the temple the entrance lies, and, taking a sword in your hand, seek out the entrance, for the opening is narrow indeed. A serpent sleeps at the entrance, guarding the temple. Seize him, and sacrifice him; skin him, and, taking his flesh and bones, dismember him. Then reunite his parts with his bones at the entrance to the temple, and, making a step of him, climb up and enter; you will find there that which you seek. The priest, this man of copper, whom you will see seated in the spring, mustering his colour, should not be thought of as a man of copper, for he has changed the colour of his nature and become a man of silver. If you wish, you will soon have him as a man of gold.[3]

The vision described has far more power than that of a mere chemical experiment put into colourful terms. For alchemists, what is true on a physical, or chemical level, is also true at the emotional and spiritual level, and their goal is to achieve transformation on all three levels at once. Thus it becomes clear why the language of dreams and visions is such an appropriate medium for alchemy, for the symbols can contain these different levels of meaning simultaneously.

Another well-known alchemical vision is that of George Ripley, who lived in the fifteenth century. In *The Twelve Gates* he wrote:

When busie at my Book I was upon a certain Night,
This *Vision* here exprest appear'd unto my dimmed
  sight:
A Toad full Ruddy I saw, did drink the juice of Grapes
  so fast,
Till over-charged with the broth, his Bowels all to brast:
And after that, from poyson'd Bulk he cast his Venom
  fell,
For Grief and Pain whereof his Members all began to
  swell;
With drops of poysoned sweat approaching thus his
  secret Den,
His Cave with blasts of fumous Air he all bewhited
  then:
And from the which in space a Golden Humour did
  ensue,

27

Whose falling drops from high did stain the soyl with
   ruddy hue.
And when his Corps the force of vital breath began
   to lack,
This dying Toad became forthwith like Coal for
   colour Black:
Thus drowned in his proper veins of poysoned flood;
For term of Eighty days and Four he rotting stood
By Tryal then this Venom to expel I did desire;
For which I did commit his Carkass to a gentle Fire:
Which done, a Wonder to the sight, but more to be
   rehearst;
The Toad with Colours rare through every side was
   pierc'd,
And White appear'd when all the sundry hews were
   past:
Which after being tincted Ruddy, for evermore did last.
Then of the Venom handled thus a Medicine I did make;
Which Venom kills, and saveth such as Venom chance to
   take:
Glory be to him the granter of such secret ways,
Dominion, and Honour both, with Worship, and with
   Praise.

                                                    AMEN.

The alchemical process is unfolded through this sequence. The first matter, the Toad (an image which is
in accordance with the idea that the primal material
may be despised and rejected by men because of its
outer appearance), is fed with alchemical water until
it bursts (separates) and releases its spirit while the
body putrefies (the nigredo). Then it is reheated and
the 'Peacock's Tail' stage of many colours occurs, being
followed by whitening and then reddening, which is the
formation of the Tincture, or Stone.

   Perhaps it may seem too neat that a fully-fledged
symbolic account of the alchemical process should arise
in George Ripley's head as he pored over his books. It
may indeed be true that the alchemist artistically shaped
his or her dreams to present a more coherent picture
of their intrinsic meaning, especially in a literary
context. However, such dreams and visions were states for

which these practitioners actively strove, and we know now that, asleep or awake, it is possible to have some measure of control over the progress of a dream, both in inducing it and in influencing its direction. 'Lucid dreaming' has been rediscovered and recognised by pschologists of today, although the faculty has existed since time immemorial and been practised in various traditions and cultures. While asleep, the subject may be aware that he or she is dreaming, and can make active choices about its development. This can give access to a more powerful level of imagery, and may also create more of a 'story' within the dream, engendered by a combination of spontaneous imagination, awareness, and active intention. A guide figure is a common feature of such dreams, and the dreamer may be encouraged to question and to follow the guide for the purpose of gaining deeper knowledge. The main difference between the alchemical and the psychological outlook is that the psychologist would see dream content as giving insight into patterns and events in the dreamer's own life, whereas the alchemist perceives the flow of imagery as emblems of occult truth, the secrets of creation explained in symbolic form.

Additionally, dreams may be encouraged to unfold while one is awake. Again, this technique has been known for centuries but is only now re-emerging into general awareness; it is often called 'guided imagery' or 'visualisation'. The imaginative faculty is allowed to work as internal vision, either moving freely or else focusing on a set theme, such as following a pathway, visiting a garden, entering a castle, and so on. A certain level of awareness must persist, or else images disintegrate into fragmented day-dreams; this is why the exercise is often carried out in groups, or with a trained leader. Images that arise this way often have much of the stirring quality of dream imagery, but without its confusion.

It is probable that alchemists took the pursuit of vision to this active stage. Ripley, it may be noted, said that his sight was 'dimmed' but not that he was sleeping. Even more telling are the words of John Dastin, whose alchemical poem, *Dastin's Dream*, begins:

Not yet full sleeping, nor yet full waking,
But between the twain lying in a trance;
Halfe closed mine Eyes in my slumbering . . .
Towards Aurora, ere Phoebus uprise,
I dreamed one came to me to do me pleasaunce
That brought me a book with seven seals close . . .

Following upon I had a wonderful dream,
As seemed to my inward thought,
The face of him shone as the sun beam:
Which unto me this heavenly book brought,
Of so great riches that it may not be bought.

The visions of the alchemists, it would seem, might occur in sleep, semi-consciousness or the waking state, sometimes triggered by long hours spent poring over books or prolonged periods of concentration as they watched the alchemical vessels for signs of change. Some may have come unbidden, as welcome but unexpected revelations which brought the insight that was needed; others may have been induced deliberately.

To whom or to what did the alchemists ascribe their visions? They knew that what they saw and experienced came from a greater source of power than that of their own imaginations. Many gladly gave thanks to God for the illumination they had received. But many also perceived a guide or spirit who acted as a medium for the vision. The author of the Hermetic text obtained his knowledge from Poimandres, 'the Mind of the Sovereignty', who was perceived as a great being. Another work, dating from the Arabic period of alchemy, but possibly having earlier origins, is entitled *The Book of Thirty Chapters*, and here the vision is granted by an unnamed being, possibly Hermes Trismegistus (the 'patron saint' of alchemy):

When I realized that love of the Great Work had fallen into my heart and that the preoccupations I felt about it had chased sleep from my eyes, that they prevented me from eating and drinking so that my body was wasting away and my appearance was bad, I gave myself up to prayer and fasting. I begged God to drive out the miseries and cares that had taken hold of my heart, and put an end to the perplexed situation in which I found myself.

While I lay asleep on my couch, a being appeared to me in a dream and told me, 'Rise up and understand what I am going to show you.'

I rose up and went off with this person. Soon we arrived before Seven Gates so fine that I had never seen the like. 'Here,' my guide said to me, 'are found the treasures of the science you seek.'

'Thank you,' I replied. 'Now guide me so that I may penetrate into these dwellings where you say are found the treasures of the universe.'

'You will never penetrate there,' he answered, 'unless you have in your power the keys of those doors. But come with me. I'll show you the keys of those doors.'

Each door corresponds to a metal associated with a planet and the aspirant is given teaching at each one. (The notion of seven gates to be passed through is strongly reminiscent of the Mithraic tradition, where initiates had to pass through seven realms ruled by planets in order to return to the source of all creation.) He is taught the relationship between body, soul and spirit, and between the elements, and is instructed in many other aspects of alchemy through word and emblem. Finally, another guide, an old man, shows him a three-bodied animal, the 'Key of Science', whose parts devour one another.

The old man said to me, 'Man, go and find that animal, give him an intelligence in place of yours, a vital spirit in place of yours, a life in place of yours; then he'll submit to you and give you all you need.'

As I wondered how I could give anyone an intelligence in place of mine, a vital spirit in place of mine, an existence in place of mine, the old man said, 'Take the body that is like your own, take from it what I have just told you, and hand it over to him.'

I did as the old man bade me, and I acquired then the whole science, as complete as that described by Hermes.[4]

Zosimos formulated a philosophy of revelation, suggesting that there was a universal being of man, with body, soul and spirit, and that it is this 'Great Man' who comes in various guises to teach the individual:

> In effect the Nous, our god, declares: 'The Son of God, who can do all things and become all things as he wishes, shows himself as he wishes to each man.
>
> And up to this day, and on till the end of the world, in secret and in hidden ways, he comes to those who are his and communicates with them, counselling them, in secret and by means of their intellect, to separate themselves from their Adam,* who blinds them and who grudges the spiritual and luminous man.'

Nicholas Flamel, a fourteenth-century alchemist saw his guiding light as an angel, who appeared to him while he was in a deep sleep, showing him an ancient, handsome volume, and telling him that he would one day understand its contents. Later he found this very book on sale and discovered it to be an old alchemical manuscript.

One of the most curious alchemical stories in which the aspirant seeks guidance comes from the pen of Bolos, a Greek alchemist. He tells us that his teacher Ostanes died before his instruction was completed. Bolos decided to summon up the spirit of his worthy master, and succeeding in this, he demanded further alchemical information from him. Ostanes remained silent during this badgering, and only when addressed more respectfully did he choose to speak, telling Bolos, 'The books are in the temple'. Bolos and his fellow students searched the temple thoroughly but found nothing. Some time later, they were enjoying a banquet in the temple when suddenly one of the columns split open. They rushed to see if the sacred tomes were hidden inside, but found only one simple formula inscribed there: 'A nature is delighted by another nature, a nature conquers another nature, a nature dominates another nature.' This, said Bolos, gave them the key to the alchemical art; the saying was also held in great reverence by later alchemists.

*Adam is the base and ignorant aspect of man.

It is clear from the alchemical accounts that the Great Work was seen as having a divine origin, and that it was thought necessary to obtain teaching through a great sage, living or dead, or through a direct vision that would serve as a basis for the work. It is little wonder, then, that we find gods, goddesses, Biblical and mythical sages claimed as founders of the art. Perhaps the boldest claim is that God gave 'the medicine' to Adam, and that it was passed from him to the chosen few who have perpetuated a line of succession. In the early days of alchemy, it was often implied that the perfect knowledge of alchemy could be found hidden in one very special book, or inscribed on a column in a certain temple. Sometimes the all-important text was thought to be hidden in the tomb of a king. Alchemists from the fifteenth to the seventeenth century in Europe dwelt on the same theme, but usually expressed it in terms of the constant search by the student for the one right book among the hundreds of fraudulent and mendacious texts available. It is the myth of the perfect knowledge, once known, and then nearly lost, lingering still in an obscure, secret or hidden place. But the knowledge is never found except through the Divine Will:

> Our Art, its theory as well as its practice, is altogether a gift of God, Who gives it when and to whom He elects . . . Though I had diligently studied this Art for seventeen or eighteen years, yet I had, after all, to wait for God's own time, and accept it as a free gift. No one need doubt the truth or certainty of this Art. It is as true and certain, and as surely ordained by God in nature, as it is that the sun shines at noon-tide, and the moon shews forth her soft splendour at night.[5]

In the later centuries of alchemy, especially in the sixteenth and seventeenth centuries, there seem to be fewer accounts of direct visions, perhaps because alchemical authors of this period were keen to introduce more philosophical discourse into their works. But the visionary quality lived on, and was often deliberately introduced in the form of parables or allegories, as in the lengthy Chymical Wedding of Christian Rosenkreutz (see p. 49). Or in A Subtle Allegory concerning the Secrets of

Alchemy, by Michael Maier which was described – truly for once – as 'very useful to possess and pleasant to read'. It tells the story of a traveller in search of the miraculous Phoenix that would change grief and anger to gold. And some of the famous sequences of visual images and commentaries, such as *The Book of Lambspring*, retain the fresh and spontaneous quality of dream symbolism.

It may be that alchemical accounts of visions have had a wider influence in the field of literature, and that other writers found in this visionary form a framework for their allegories. We will see in Chapter Five how the visionary aspect of alchemy may have influenced the early forms of opera. Langland's *Piers Plowman*, written in the four-teenth century, begins with the narration of Piers as he falls asleep by the side of the stream: 'And I dreamt a marvellous dream: I was in a wilderness, I could not tell where, and looking Eastwards I saw a tower high up against the sun, and splendidly built on top of a hill; and far beneath it was a great gulf, with a dungeon in it, surrounded by deep, dark pits, dreadful to see . . .' Even closer to the alchemical genre is John Bunyan's *Pilgrim's Progress* (1675), which traces the journey of the pilgrim who wishes to reach salvation and charts the crises and stages of transformation he must go through before reaching the Holy City. It starts: 'As I walked through the wilderness of this world, I lighted on a certain place where there was a den, and laid me down in that place to sleep; and as I slept, I dreamed a dream . . .' It has a great deal in common with the alchemical process, since it begins with Christian's struggle with the Slough of Despond, the 'scum and filth' of the world, that equates with the base First Matter of the alchemists. It ends, as does the Great Work, with gold, in the Celestial City:

> So I saw that when they awoke [Christian and Hope] they addressed themselves to go up to the city. But, as I said, the reflection of the sun upon the city (for the city was pure gold . . .) was so extremely glorious, that they could not, as yet, with open faces behold it, but through an instrument made for that purpose. So I saw that, as they went on, there met them two men in raiment that shone like gold, also their faces shone as the light . . .

4 · EMBLEMS OF KNOWLEDGE

Alchemy passed from the Greeks and Egyptians to the Arabs, by whom it was then transmitted to Europe. From the seventh century onwards, the Arabs devoted much time and study not only to alchemy but also to mathematics, astronomy and astrology. The rise of the new religion, Islam, founded by the prophet Mohammed, gave a strong focus for the Arab tribes and enabled them to consolidate their identity; from this new unity arose conditions favourable to learning and experiment. The Arabs expanded their Islamic Empire into Spain in the eighth century, and this, though it was the cause of strife, enabled Arabic teachings and ideas to pass more easily into the rest of Europe.

The Arabs translated many ancient alchemical works from the Greek, and certain Greek texts have come down to us today only through their Arabic versions, making it difficult for scholars to verify and date the original material. The most famous Arabian alchemists known to us are Khalid ibn Yazid (d. 704), Abu Musa Jabir (fl. 760), and Al-Razi (b. *c* 864). **Khalid** was a prince who lived at Damascus, said to have been the first Moslem to take an interest in alchemy and to have been initiated into its secrets by a Christian hermit called Morienus.

Jabir, often called **Geber**, was venerated by the later European alchemists more than any other Arabic writer, and it is probable that a Geber school or tradition carried on his work and used his name to head later texts. Abu Musa Jabir lived in the eighth century; he was a member of a South Arabian tribe who came to Arabia from Persia because of political unrest. It is said that he studied with certain important religious leaders of the day and that he became a Sufi, a member of that mystical and esoteric sect that flourished within Islam. As well as alchemy, he studied medicine, warfare and music, and we know that he found favour at court for much of his life as a respected scholar. His most influential ideas were probably those that modified the Aristotelian theory of the elements.

Geber also introduced some of the Arabian love of numbers into alchemy. He worked out various complicated systems for calculating the right amounts of materials and substances to use in alchemical procedures. He attempted to find the perfect balance of substances and elements and came nearer to the modern principles of chemical equations in his work than any other alchemist of this or later times. About a hundred books are ascribed to him, but it is certain that many of these are pseudographical. Some of the alchemical methods he describes are so complex and tortuous that his name gave rise to the term 'gibberish'. There is a legend that about two hundred years after his death his laboratory at Kufa was discovered as some houses were being demolished, exposing his work room, and a golden mortar more than two pounds in weight!

Al-Rhazi, also known as **Rhases**, was born around AD 864, and spent his life chiefly at Ray, near Teheran, with periods of work carried out at Baghdad. He is remembered as a man of great learning, specialising in medicine and alchemy, but also noted for his understanding of philosophy and for his skill as a musician. His writings on medicine stood the test of time until the sixteenth or seventeenth century, and in his day he was surrounded by many young students and visiting scholars whom he instructed. E. J. Holmyard quotes the following description of his teaching life:

One of his biographers has drawn a graphic picture of Razi as an old man, seated on the paving of the courtyard of the hospital surrounded by his pupils. The advanced students sat in a ring nearest him, and in outer concentric rings sat those whom we might call the second-year and first-year men. Razi, the fount of wisdom at the centre, expounded to his immediate entourage, and the information, suitably simplified, was passed on to the less experienced.[1]

His works were great favourites with the European alchemists, even though he was interested primarily in practical chemistry, especially in the classification of substances and in improving laboratory technique.

THE ALCHEMICAL OPERATION

Early European alchemists seized eagerly upon any translations they could acquire of Arabian and Greek alchemical texts. But for them by far and away the most significant early text was the *Emerald Tablet of Hermes Trismegistus*, also called the *Tabula Smaragdina*. This was the alchemists' creed, the affirmation of their work, and a constant source of guidance and wisdom to them. It was sometimes engraved on the walls of the alchemical laboratory, and there can scarcely have been an alchemist who did not have the words written out or committed to memory.

There are several versions of the text, since it is known both in Latin and Arabic, and probably existed in Syriac and Greek forms before that. The translation commonly favoured by present-day scholars is that of R. Steele and D. W. Singer, made earlier this century, which runs as follows:

True it is, without falsehood, certain and most true. That which is above is like to that which is below, and that which is below is like to that which is above, to accomplish the miracles of one thing.

And as all things were by the contemplation of one, so all things arose from this one thing by a single act of adaptation.

The father thereof is the Sun, the mother the Moon.

Fig. 2 'The father thereof is the Sun, the mother the Moon', as the Emerald Tablet states. Conception takes place in the alchemical bath. (From Atlanta Fugiens by Michael Maier.)

The Wind carried it in its womb, the Earth is the nurse thereof.

It is the father of all works of wonder throughout the whole world.

The power thereof is perfect.

If it be cast on to Earth, it will separate the element of Earth from that of Fire, the subtle from the gross.

With great sagacity it doth ascend gently from Earth to Heaven.

Again it doth descend to Earth, and uniteth in itself the force from things superior and things inferior.

Thus thou wilt possess the glory of the brightness of the whole world, and all obscurity will fly from thee.

This thing is the strong fortitude of all strength, for it overcometh every subtle thing and doth penetrate every solid substance.

Thus was this world created.

Hence will there be marvellous adaptations achieved, of which the manner is this.

For this reason I am called Hermes Trismegistus, because I hold three parts of the wisdom of the whole world.

That which I had to say about the operation of Sol is completed.

It is likely that this text originates from the early centuries of the Christian era, in common with other writings ascribed to Hermes (see p. 92). But the European alchemists believed that the words came from the very dawn of time, and were the original revelation of alchemy to man through the divine person of Hermes Trismegistus. 'Hermes saw the totality of things. Having seen he understood. Having understood, he had the power to reveal and show. And indeed what he knew, he wrote down. What he wrote, he mostly hid away, keeping silence rather than speaking out, so that every generation coming into the world had to seek out these things.'[2]

The name Hermes Trismegistus means Hermes the Thrice Great. In the general evolution of the classical deities, Hermes later became known as Mercury; but though Hermes and Mercury play somewhat similar roles in alchemy, they are not identical. Hermes was seen as the source of alchemical knowledge and was often thought to have been a real, though semi-divine, Egyptian adept. Mercury was the representation of the living spirit of alchemy, the volatile transforming power that could exalt matter into its most refined state; we shall return to him shortly.

The enigmatic character of the Emerald Tablet, and indeed the trickster qualities of Hermes and Mercury, are reflected in alchemical literature of all periods. Alchemical texts and illustrations are fascinating, but they are also tantalising, cryptic, and sometimes deliberately misleading in their descriptions. How true the alchemical aphorism: 'Many search; few find'. Sometimes, even if the secret could be found, it was too late; after working for sixty years, the aged seeker, Tonsile, met an initiate only to be rebuffed thus:

> Tonsile said I, what should it you avail
> Such a thing to know? your limbs doth you fail
> For very age, therefore cease your lay;
> And love your beads, it is high time to pray;
> For if you knew the materials of our stone
> Ere you could make it your days would be gone.[3]

The influence of the Arabian alchemists may well be felt in the labelling of the stages of the process which these medieval and later European alchemists used. As well as emblematic pictures and mythological descriptions, the stages were given titles relating more closely to the chemical operations that were carried out. These act as a reminder that alchemy had a nitty gritty physical side to it, however important the spiritual process. *The Sum of Perfection*, attributed to Geber, but probably by an early medieval author, lists the stages as: sublimation, descension, distillation, calcination, solution, coagulation, fixation and ceration. These involve processes we would recognise in physical terms as heating, condensation, evaporation, and so on. Lest it should be thought that with one such key we have swiftly arrived at the heart of the alchemical secret, it should be immediately pointed out that no two such descriptions of the process ever agreed! Even the number of stages varied, often set between seven and twelve, linking in to other symbolic correspondences such as the seven days of creation or the twelve signs of the zodiac. George Ripley, a fifteenth century alchemist, called the operation *The Twelve Gates* and likened it to a circular castle with twelve entrances, each signifying a stage of the process. These were named as: calcination, solution, separation, conjunction, putrefaction, congelation, cibation, sublimation, fermentation, exaltation, multiplication and projection. We can make connections between the chemical and symbolical significance of some of these, for instance the conjunction signifying combining sulphur and mercury in the vessel and the marriage of the king and queen. Putrefaction, the stage that follows, indicates that the united bodies must be killed by heat so that regeneration may follow, which corresponds to the death, the blackening, whose symbol is the raven.

THE PRIMAL MATERIAL

The alchemist must take some substance to start his operations. But what should his 'first matter' be? This is one of the most jealously guarded secrets of alchemy. However, since the perfect Stone is to be created from something that is apparently base and worthless, the matter required is often described as being overlooked and despised by men – 'the corner stone which the builders rejected'. The baser forms of alchemy, especially in the Middle Ages, took this as a sign that any particularly nasty substance would do, such as 'poudres diverse, asshes, dong, pisse, and cley' (Chaucer, *The Canon Yeoman's Tale*), not to mention blood, hair, bones and spittle. The more sophisticated alchemists poured scorn upon this practice, and implied that the first material is no common substance, but a mysterious ingredient of the universe. It is:

> familiar to all men, both young and old, is found in the country, in the village, in the town, in all things created by God; yet it is despised by all. Rich and poor handle it every day. It is cast into the street by servant maids. Children play with it. Yet no one prizes it, though, next to the human soul, it is the most beautiful and the most precious thing upon earth and has the power to pull down kings and princes. Nevertheless, it is esteemed the vilest and meanest of earthly things.[4]

Some authorities consider that in the early days of alchemy, the black Egyptian silt with its tremendous fertility may have provided the idea of a base substance with great nourishing and creative powers. Whether or not this is true, by the sixteenth and seventeenth centuries, the concept had become much more complex. Some writers imply that the primal material is metallic, because it is impossible to create gold from anything that does not have a metallic root; but they also hint that its form does not resemble what we usually think of as metal. And in some texts the distinction between the *prima materia* and the Stone itself, the end product of the process, is hard to define; the implication seems to be that the Stone is released from the base material by the alchemical process and is already indwelling in it when the alchemist takes it up:

> This Matter is found in one thing, out of which alone our Stone is prepared ... without any foreign admixture; and its quality, appearance, and properties have been set forth in the following manner. It is composed of three things, yet it is only *one* ... They also call it the universal Magnesia, or the seed of the world, from which all natural objects take their origin. Its properties are of a singular kind; for, in addition to its marvellous nature and form, it is neither hot and dry like fire, nor cold and wet like water, nor cold and dry like earth, but a perfect preparation of all the elements ... With respect to its outward appearance, figure, form, and shape, they call it a stone, and not a stone ... It is found *potentially* everywhere, and in everything, but in all its perfection and fullness only in *one* thing ... By the ignorant and the beginner it is thought to be the vilest and meanest of things. It is sought by many Sages, and found by few; suspected by those that are far away, and received by those that are near; seen by all, but known by few ...[5]

It is also associated with the Ouroboros, the circular serpent with its tail in its mouth. This goes back to the dawn of alchemy, for in an early Greek text we read:

> Here is the mystery: The serpent Ouroboros [biting his tail] is the composition which in our [work] is devoured and melted, dissolved and transformed by fermentation. It becomes dark green from which the golden colour derives. It is from this which the red comes, called the colour of cinnabar; it is the cinnabar of the philosophers.
>
> Its stomach and its back are the colour of saffron; its head is dark green, its four legs are the four imperfect metals [lead, copper, tin, iron]; its three ears are the three sublimated vapours [perhaps salt, mercury and sulphur].
>
> The One gives to the Other its blood; and the One engenders the Other. Nature rejoices in nature; nature charms nature; nature triumphs over nature; and nature masters nature; and this is not from one nature opposing

another, but through the one and same nature, through the alchemical process, with care and great effort.[6]

In the *Gold Making of Cleopatra* (*c.* AD 100) the Ouroboros is drawn and the text reads: 'One is the All and by it the All and in it the All and if it does not contain the All it is nothing.' Although the later alchemists, especially in the seventeenth century, brought the philosophy of their work to the heights of sophistication, yet they still based their operations on the simplicity and unity of this premise. Transformation comes primarily through purifying and perfecting the original material. This is a declaration of faith, that the divine spark dwells in every single atom that exists, however corrupt and base it may appear to our eyes.

MERCURY

The alchemical serpent, or dragon, is closely connected with Mercury, the transforming agent of the alchemical process. Mercury is released and activated from the primal material, and is then transformed, fixed, and brought to perfection through the operations. Appropriately enough for such an elusive and volatile figure, alchemical descriptions of him – or her, for it is often stated that the Mercurial force is a feminine one – blend into definitions of the first material, the Stone, and 'our gold'. 'Our Mercury' is not 'common mercury', the alchemists are quick to point out. Charles Nicholl, in *The Chemical Theatre*, grapples with these problems admirably:

> There are two directions in which alchemical Mercury leads us. On the one hand, it is a complex elaboration of chemical substance, its various qualities referring back to the properties of quicksilver, or 'common mercury' . . . But there is another direction entirely, away from chemical matter. Mercury is not, finally, a substance, or even many substances: it is a process . . . All these [alchemical writings] point to one crucial idea: that transformation is something intrinsic and contained *inside* matter . . . Each stage of this self-devouring, self-generating process bears the name 'Mercury'. Mercury, in short, is alchemy itself.

*Fig. 3   Mercury is sometimes described as a double agent.
Here the two Mercuries must be joined, like with like,
according to alchemical principles.
(From Atlanta Fugiens by Michael Maier.)*

In his *Alchemical Studies*, C. G. Jung quotes from *Aurelia Occulta*, which is contained in the *Theatrum Chemicum*:

> I am the poison-dripping dragon, who is everywhere and
> can be cheaply had. That upon which I rest, and that
> which rests upon me, will be found within me by those
> who pursue their investigations in accordance with the
> rules of the Art. My water and fire destroy and put
> together; from my body you may extract the green lion
> and the red. But if you do not have exact knowledge
> of me, you will destroy your five senses with my fire.
> From my snout there comes a spreading poison that has
> brought death to many. Therefore you should skilfully
> separate the coarse from the fine, if you do not wish

to suffer utter poverty. I bestow on you the powers of the male and the female, and also those of heaven and of earth. The mysteries of my art must be handled with courage and greatness of mind if you would conquer me by the power of fire, for already very many have come to grief, their riches and labour lost. I am the egg of nature, known only to the wise ... By the philosophers I am named Mercurius; my spouse is the [philosophic] gold; I am the old dragon, found everywhere on the globe of the earth, father and mother, young and old, very strong and very weak, death and resurrection, visible and invisible, hard and soft; I descend into the earth and ascend to the heavens, I am the highest and the lowest, the lightest and the heaviest; often the order of nature is reversed in me, as regards colour, number, weight and measure; I contain the light of nature; I am dark and light; I come forth from heaven and earth; I am known and yet do not exist at all; by virtue of the sun's rays all colours shine in me and all metals. I am the carbuncle of the sun, the most noble purified earth, through which you may change copper, iron, tin, and lead into gold.

On a lighter note, Mercury can be found in conversation with an alchemist in *The New Chemical Light* by Michael Sendivogius.[7] A foolish alchemist has read that he should start his work with Mercury; he tries to heat common quicksilver which evaporates, where upon he accuses his wife of stealing it. Then he tries again, adding all sorts of substances to it such as 'herbs, urine and vinegar' to see if he can do any better. Failing with these, he remembers reading that the dung hill is the place to seek, so he starts to use dung, but all ends badly. Then, in a dream, a wise old man tells him to use the 'Mercury of the Sages'. He manages to conjure up Mercury in person, and tries to wrest the secret from him, but Mercury, true to form, is mischievous and avoids all the alchemist's attempts to force him into submission:

Alchemist: I conjure you by the living God – are you not the Mercury of the Sages? *Mercury* (pretending to speak in a whimpering and frightened tone of voice): Master, I *am* Mercury. *Alchemist*: Why would you not obey me then? Why could I not fix you? *Mercury*: Oh, most high and mighty Master, I implore you to spare your miserable slave! I did not know that you were such a potent philosopher. *Alchemist*: Oh, could you not guess as much from the philosophical way in which I operated on you . . . (To the Mercury, in awful tones of thunder): Now mind that you obey me, else it will be the worse for you. *Mercury*: Gladly, Master, if I can: for I am very weak. *Alchemist*: Oho, do you begin to make excuses already? *Mercury*: No, but I am very languid. *Alchemist*: What is the matter with you? *Mercury*: An Alchemist is the matter with me. *Alchemist*: Are you laughing at me, you false rogue? *Mercury*: Oh, no, no, Master, as God shall spare me, I spoke of an Alchemist – you are a philosopher . . . *Alchemist*: Well, I won't praise myself, but I certainly am a learned man. My wife says so too. She always calls me a profoundly learned philosopher. *Mercury*: I quite believe you. For philosophers are men whom too much learning and thought have made mad. *Alchemist*: Tell me, what am I to do with you? How am I to make you into the Philosopher's Stone? *Mercury*: Oh, my master philosopher, that I cannot tell. You are a philosopher, I am the philosopher's humble slave. Whatever he wishes to make me, I become, as far as my nature will allow. *Alchemist*: That is all very fine, but I repeat that you must tell me how to treat you, and whether you can become the Philosopher's Stone. *Mercury*: Mr Philosopher, if you know, you can make it, and if you don't you can't . . .

ELEMENTAL SYMBOLS

We have already looked at the basic role of the four elements in alchemy, and the qualities associated with them. Their specific functions in alchemy, however, though often obscure and mysterious, have interesting images and associations attached to them. The most important ideas concerning earth have been considered in the section on the Primal Material, but earth may also be represented by creatures such as the deer and the unicorn. Fishes are the creatures of water, birds of air, and salamanders of fire. Fire is mainly an external force in alchemy; the alchemist tends his furnace scrupulously, and must apply the right degree of heat for the different stages of the operation. Often the heat is to be moderate, like that of a chicken giving warmth to her eggs. The period of gestation, after the 'seed' of the Stone has been engendered and remains in the tightly-sealed vessel to come to term, is sustained by the application of fire.

There are often hints that a substance undergoing transformation must yield up its secret fire, which will help to give the Stone its final power. The Salamander must be brought from his cave:

> [The Salamander] is caught and pierced
> So that it dies and yields up its life with its blood.
> But this, too, happens for its good:
> For from its blood it wins immortal life,
> And then death has no more power over it.[8]

Water is closely associated with Mercury. It is the universal solvent, and can also be considered as helping to give the right colour to the substance at different stages of the operation – black, white, yellow or red. We have already seen how colour was considered to be a kind of spirit, with special properties and powers. It is also necessary to remember that all the elements were thought to have a higher form, which was quite different from that of normal earth, water, fire and air, and it is probably these special forms which are known as 'our fire' and 'our water'. 'Our Pontic and Catholic water . . . is sweet, beautiful clear, limpid, and brighter than gold, silver, carbuncles, or diamonds'; 'Our water is a water which does not wet the hands; it is a heavenly water, and yet not rain water'; 'Our water is serene, crystalline, pure and beautiful'.

A kind of water that is given particular importance in alchemical texts is dew. A famous plate from the *Mutus Liber* (1667) shows a male and a female alchemist wringing out into a bowl dew that they have gathered by exposing large sheets of cloth to the air. Dew might be used to moisten the alchemical matter, to bathe it or to nourish it. What would make dew so special? There are two schools of thought on this. Some alchemists, such as Armand Barbault, the twentieth-century French alchemist, consider dew to be permeated with the living vitality of the plants from which it is gathered; it thus imparts a 'green fire' – an enriching food – to the matter. Others see dew as descending from the atmosphere, a mystical medium, the receptacle of celestial influences. In the *Zohar* (a collection of Cabbalistic writings dating from medieval times), dew is mentioned as a holy attribute:

> *v. 47* – And it is written, Isa xxvi. 19: 'The dew of the lights is thy dew.' Of the lights – that is, from the brightness of the Ancient One.
>
> *48* – And by that dew are nourished the holy supernal ones.
>
> *49* – And this is that manna which is prepared for the just in the world to come.
>
> *50* – And that dew distilleth upon the ground of the holy apple trees . . .
>
> *51* – And the appearance of this dew is white, like unto the colour of the crystal stone, whose appearance hath all colours in itself.[9]

The element of air is related to the emblem of birds, which occur in many different forms in alchemical texts. It would be possible to devote a whole book just to the symbolism of the different birds in alchemy.[10] The appearance of the *raven* or *crow* symbolizes the *nigredo*, or putrefaction of the first material. A white bird, such as the *swan*, or *dove*, may refer to the first time that the 'soul' of the matter is released, the matter having polarized into the black of the raven and the white of the more elevated bird. The *peacock* has the quality of a herald, for with the arrival of the Peacock's Tail, the show of beautiful irridescent colours in the vessel, the alchemist knows that his work is empowered and that the transformation is under way. The *pelican* is represented in connection with the legend that the pelican fed her young with the blood of her own breast, which relates to the idea that the first matter contained in itself all that it needed for transformation and perfection, including its own nourishment: this is similar to the concept of the secret 'water' being extracted from the substance and then fed back to it to help it grow. The *eagle* has a close association with Mercury, and two eagles shown fighting each other refer to the internal battle that takes place in the initial stages to untie the knot which binds the elements together. The eagle exalted or poised in the air is Mercury in his most sublime state, emblem of inspiration and knowledge, frequently a sign that the work is completed.

In *The Chemical Wedding of Christian Rosenkreutz* (1690), a long alchemical allegory concerning an initiate's quest to be accepted and present at a royal wedding, there is a description of the alchemical process in terms of a bird that emerges from an egg, changes colour and shape, and is sacrificed for its blood:

> Our Egg being now ready was taken out; But it needed no cracking, for the Bird that was in it soon freed himself, and shewed himself very jocond, yet he looked very Bloody and unshapen: ... The Bird grew so fast under our eyes, that we well saw why the Virgin gave us such a warning of him. He bit and scratcht so devillishly about him, that could he have had his will upon any of us, he would have soon dispatched him. Now he was wholly black, and wild, wherefore other meat was brought to him ... whereupon all his black Feathers moulted again, and instead of them there grew out Snow-white Feathers. He was somewhat tamer too, and suffered himself to be more tractable, nevertheless we did not trust him. At the third feeding his Feathers began to be so curiously coloured, that in all my Life I never saw the like colours for Beauty. He was also exceeding tame, and behaved himself so friendly with us, that (the Virgin consenting) we released him from his Captivity.

The images and symbols of alchemy helped to show the profundity of the alchemical operation. The alchemist saw his work as a great mystery, as a way of penetrating to the heart of the created world. He took nothing for granted; he did not treat his laboratory operations as mechanical repetitions but as a living process in which he must participate. He aimed to go beyond the realm of normal appearances and effects, to the causes of those effects, where he might glimpse 'Venus unveiled' in her chamber – an experience so intense and powerful that it was considered highly dangerous if the alchemist was not inwardly prepared. An analogous situation might be if the atomic physicist suddenly began to experience and perceive everything at the atomic level. Normal concepts of solidity, shape and identity would cease to have meaning; it is not difficult to see that the experience could be a totally overwhelming unless one was prepared and trained for it, emotionally and mentally, irrespective of how much 'atomic theory' one knew in advance.

THE CELESTIAL INFLUENCE

The relationship of the earth to the solar system and to the stars was considered very important in alchemy. In fact, until the eighteenth century, it was accepted by the majority of people that the celestial bodies were animate and possessed of particular qualities that affected life on earth. The accompanying assumption was that they were instruments, or agents of the Divine Will, and sometimes (more immediately) the tools of Nature, governing the growth of everything upon earth, including metals. The following quotation indicates the power of Nature and the part played by the planets:

> By my wisdom I govern the first principle of motion. My hands are the eighth sphere, as my Father ordained; my hammers are the seven planets with which I forge beautiful things. The substance out of which I fashion all my works, and all things under heaven, I obtain from the four elements alone . . . By my virtue and efficacy I make the imperfect perfect, whether it be a metal or a human body. I mix its ingredients, and temper the four elements. I reconcile opposites, and calm their Discord.
>
> This is the golden chain which I have linked together of my heavenly virtues and earthly substances.[11]

Each metal was said to correspond to a particular planet, and when that planet was strong in influence, the 'growth' of the metal would be accelerated within the earth. The influence could be assessed astrologically, by examining the relationship of the planets to one another and studying their position in relation to the signs of the zodiac for the time in question. The association of planets with metals was precise, and related to the active principle of the planet as defined astrologically or mythologically. Saturn, for instance, considered to be slow, profound, weighty, had the correspondence of lead, the heaviest of the metals concerned. Venus, planet of ease, pleasure, beauty and malleability, corresponded to copper, a soft and gleaming metal. The sun corresponded to gold, the moon to silver, Mercury to quicksilver, Mars to iron, and Jupiter to tin. The alchemist would need to know and understand these correspondences well, since it was common to try and prepare elixirs of the other metals apart from silver and gold, especially as medicinal remedies. Often in the alchemical texts one will find the metals called by the names of the planets themselves.

Since Nature was said to operate through the medium of the planets, the alchemist, seeking to use art to accelerate and perfect the natural processes, must understand and utilise the principles of stellar influences. Many alchemists, therefore, were skilled astrologers, and it was common to select a favourable time astrologically to begin the Great Work. The initiation of new stages of the process might also be governed by astrological conditions. It was generally considered that the work was best begun at or around the vernal equinox, when the sun moves into the sign of Aries, the first point of the Zodiac. However, more elaborate calculations and assessments were frequently employed, just as a gardener might have it in mind to sow certain seeds in a particular week, but would vary the timing according to prevalent weather and ground conditions.

Alchemists perpetuated the view that the cosmos is whole and alive and that all its components have spirit and purpose; the stars and the planets provide a 'field' of energy that man can either experience passively or use actively for creative purposes. The alchemist therefore cannot work against the natural and stellar influences, but he can channel them to bring about transformation:

Let me sum up in a few words what I have to say. The substance is of heavenly birth, its life is preserved by the stars, and nourished by the four elements; then it must perish, and be putrefied; again, by the influence of the stars, which works through the elements, it is restored to life, and becomes once more a heavenly thing that has its habitation in the highest region of the firmament. Then you will find that the heavenly has assumed an earthly body, and that the earthly body has been reduced to a heavenly substance.[12]

THE ALCHEMIST: IMAGE AND REALITY

What image does the word alchemist conjure up? Perhaps that of a lean and bearded figure, dressed in a dark and dusty cloak, muttering mysterious incantations as he leans over his cauldrons and bubbling retorts. When the history of alchemy is studied, it soon becomes obvious that this picture is far from the truth, but it must also be noted that even in its heyday alchemy was considered a subject for ridicule. The majority of people were not well informed about alchemical aims and practices, partly because most serious alchemists kept very much to themselves, and those who did pronounce themselves publicly to be alchemists were often the most fraudulent or foolish practitioners of all. It is from their activities that the popular image of alchemy derives.

> Their clothes be bawdy and worn thread-bare,
> Men may smell them for multipliers where they go;
> To file their fingers with corrosives they do not spare
> Their eyes be bleryd, and their cheeks both lean
>   and blue . . .
> They search for the stone in soot, dung, urine, wine,
>   blood, eggs.
> To see their houses it is a noble sport,
> What furnaces, what glasses there be of divers shape;
> What salts, what powders, what oils, and waters fort,
> How eloquently, *de materia prima*, they clape
> And yet to find the truth they have no hap.[13]

Many came to ruin through their search for the stone, addicted to the quest for gold and spending all their time and money in fruitless experiment. The unsuccessful experimenters were characterised by a tink of brimstone,

Fig. 4   An alchemist's laboratory. Notice the caduceus shape, a physical representation of Mercury's emblem (see the illustration of the double Mercury on p. 43)

worn-out clothes, an unhealthy tinge to the skin and a general air of poverty. The charlatans could be distinguished by their bragging and boasting, their readiness to talk about the art of alchemy and their willingness to promise spectacular transmutations; they often lived a wandering life – for obvious reasons.

Going beyond the superficial picture, though, we find quite different types of people seriously involved in the study of alchemy. In medieval times these were often monks, but both then and later the aspirants included noblemen, men of business, men of learning – and a few women. All had to have enough time and money to support their researches, for there were likely to be months and even years of long experiment and the alchemist had to be committed to regulating the fire, mixing, adding, and, above all, to waiting and watching for the right reactions in the vessel.

In medieval times the monastic environment provided excellent opportunities for alchemical work. Monasteries were natural centres of learning, since all books were written in manuscript form and one of the chief occupations of monks was in copying out and illuminating the texts. Many monasteries had fine libraries, and received visitors from afar bringing new insights from other teachers and countries.

We find many traces of monastic alchemists. In Elias Ashmole's anthology of alchemical poetry (*Theatrum Chemicum Britannicum*) we find a contribution from the rather sinister-sounding 'Pearce, the Black Monk', who had a fair talent for verse, the style of which would seem to place him in the medieval period:

> I am Mercury the mighty flower,
> I am most worthy of honour;
> I am source of Sol, Luna and Mars,
> I am settler of Saturn, and source of Venus,
> I am Empress, Princess, and Regal of Queens,
> I am Mother of Mirror, and maker of light,
> I am head and highest and fairest in sight . . .

John Dastin a member of an austere monastic order, is remembered for his courageous fight to keep the name of alchemy untarnished. He lived in the first half of the fourteenth century, at a time when Pope John XXII had condemned alchemy because of the proliferation of fraudulent practitioners. He passed an edict by which those caught counterfeiting gold and silver had to repay the equivalent sum of money back into the common treasury; persistent offenders had their goods confiscated and were branded as criminals: offending clerics were to be deprived of their livings. Dastin wrote both to the Pope and to Cardinal Orsini assuring them that there was more to alchemy than deception, and maintained that it was within the possibilities of nature to prepare the alchemical elixir. The Pope may have been dazzled by such erudition; at any rate, Dastin does not seem to have suffered for his efforts; and E.J. Holmyard tells us that when the Pope died, he left an enormous fortune that was reputed to be of alchemical origin!

The most famous alchemical monk is **Sir George Ripley**, who came of an aristocratic family and was a Canon regular in the Augustinian priory at Bridlington, in Yorkshire. This priory had a strong tradition of learning and in the fifteenth century Ripley made it the base for his alchemical experiments, apparently antagonising the other inhabitants by the smells and fumes that were generated in his laboratory. One interesting feature of Ripley's alchemical education is that he spent some time in Rhodes, as a guest of the Knights of St. John of Jerusalem. Rhodes had been occupied by the Knights since 1310, and quickly gained a reputation for being a cosmopolitan centre of learning, a little like a latter-day Alexandria. The Knights' community, though based on Catholic principles, was receptive to innovatory ideas that would have been suspect elsewhere, and many came to Rhodes to teach and learn in an atmosphere of comparative intellectual freedom.

Since one of the chief occupations of the Knights of St. John was healing the sick, there was a natural connection between their endeavours to promote the study of medicine and herbalism, and alchemy, whose Elixir had the reputation of being a panacea. In the late medieval period, Jacques Millac, a French herbalist and apothecary who had antagonised the Catholic Church in his own country because of his interest in alchemy, joined the Order in order to be able to live in Rhodes and experiment as he wished. A university had been established there that was noted for its teaching of medicine, while a special school for apothecaries was attached to the hospital run by the Knights. Ripley, (in the fifteenth century) is understood to have gained at least some of his alchemical expertise during his stay on Rhodes. Another noted alchemist, **Bernard of Treves** (probably in the fourteenth century) completed his alchemical studies on Rhodes, where it is said that he met a 'man of religion' whose alchemical library was attractive enough to keep him there for eight years.

Ripley became well known for such works as *The Compound of Alchemy* (containing the famous passage on the Twelve Gates), which quickly became established as alchemical classics. With Ripley, a link is formed between the clerical and the secular alchemist, for **Thomas Norton**, a well-to-do Bristol merchant claimed that Ripley was his teacher. Norton, who may also have held the post of privy councillor to Edward IV, published his work *The Ordinall of Alchemy* anonymously in 1477. However, despite the appearance of discretion and modesty, he plainly had hopes that someone would recognise his hand in the work, as he concealed his name in an easy cipher which revealed the motto:

> Thomas Norton of Briseto
> A parfet Master ye maie him trowe.

Thomas Charnock, born around 1524, was also taught alchemy by monks. His profession is not known and he had little education, though this did not deter him from the search. His own account of his work[14] is full of zest and frankness, and he was plainly pleased with his own verse. He recounts how he meets a blind friar who tells him that he will only teach the alchemical art to a most gifted and wonderful young man that he has heard of called Charnock! His virtues are apparently such that:

> 'Wherefore his knowledge, gravity and wit,
> He may well be crowned Poet Laureate.'

Charnock suffered several set-backs in his alchemical work. The most infuriating came when he was called up to fight at Calais:

> When I saw there was none other boot
> But that I must go spite of my heart took root;
> In my fury I took a hatchet in my hand,
> And brake all my work whereas it did stand,
> And as for my pots I knocked them together,

And also my glasses into many a shiver . . .

From the sixteenth century onwards alchemy became a magnet for men of learning, especially those seeking a comprehensive knowledge of the universe. Their creed was that there should be no boundaries between arts, sciences, mysticism and occult knowledge. Each discipline was seen both as a valid way of gaining knowledge about the created world and of learning to operate within it. A metaphysical understanding would both help to explain physical phenomena and inspire practical inventions. Yet, though alchemy was taken seriously by those of considerable intellectual reputation, it certainly never found universal favour. Some were simply sceptical of alchemical claims but others saw in alchemy and occult arts the machinations of the devil.

John Dee (1527–1608), a controversial Elizabethan figure, was suspected of being a sorcerer when he invented an elaborate mechanical beetle for a stage play that gave the illusion of flying! Dee was a remarkable man who took a keen interest in alchemy; in later life he had laboratories built at his house in Mortlake. He was a favourite of Queen's Elizabeth, who consulted him as to a suitable astrological date and time for her coronation. Dee was well versed in mechanics, optics, navigation, history and mathematics and was far-sighted enough to propose a national scheme for the preservation of ancient monuments and a national 'Library Royal'. He took a special interest in clairvoyance and is often remembered for his association with the dubious Edward Kelley, who acted as a scryer for him in his attempts to communicate with the world of spirits and angels. But, Dee was not the unquestioning dupe that some authorities have assumed, for his diaries show that he was often critical of Kelley. However, he found certain qualities or psychic abilities in Kelley that he valued, and together they tried both crystal gazing and dowsing for hidden treasure. Dee and Kelley went to Poland together, where they undertook to demonstrate alchemical transformation to the Emperor of Bohemia; but the attempt failed and they were dismissed in a state of near poverty after which they parted company.

WOMEN IN ALCHEMY

Women have played a less prominent part in alchemy than men. Plainly, the demands of an art that required constant and prolonged attention made it impossible for most women to pursue it seriously, for it would

Fig. 5   The Dragon must be slain to release its vital powers.
(From Atlanta Fugiens *by Michael Maier.)*

not fit in easily with childbearing or with the running of a household. However, certain women alchemists are known to have existed; some husbands and wives worked together, and it is possible that further research would bring to light accounts of more women who were interested in alchemy. We have already seen that Maria the Jewess and Kleopatra were noted alchemists of antiquity. Zosimos, the Greek alchemist, had a sister called Theosebeia who was involved in alchemy, but we only know of her existence through fragments of letters that Zosimos wrote to her. Later times have no well-known lady alchemists on record, but it is possible that they were overlooked both by historians and contemporary alchemists. There are a few brief references: John Aubrey (the seventeenth-century historian) mentions that Mary Sidney (the wife of the Earl of Pembroke) was 'a great chymist, and spent yearly a great deale in that study'. Lady Anne Conway (1642–1684) has already been cited as being highly influential in the Rosicrucian circle of the period, whose members would have included alchemy as one of their chief studies.

A theme that is shadowy to unravel, but in some ways more interesting to contemplate, is of man and woman working together in 'the Great Work'. The process of alchemy depends upon correct understanding of the male and female principles inherent in matter (sulphur and mercury), of separating them and uniting them in harmony, and it is therefore readily understandable that the alchemists would have sought to echo this idea in their own work. In certain pictures and accounts we find the idea that both the man and the woman had something vital to contribute to the operation. Illustrations in the *Liber Mutus* (1677) show a man and a woman working together to gather dew, tend the vessel and the furnace, and assist each other in almost every stage of the process. The illustrations show precisely the different actions performed by each of the pair. In one illustration, they kneel on each side of the furnace; the man has his hands folded and his head bowed in prayer while the woman gazes upwards, lifting one arm high in a graceful gesture of blessing. Armand Barbault, a noted twentieth-century alchemist, always worked in conjunction with a female partner, and has this to say about the role of the man and the woman in the operation:

> Through her extreme sensibility and the mobility of her own bodily fluids, the woman is to a certain extent in a favourable position to cross to higher levels and so receive instructions for her partner. His role, on the other hand, is far more earth-bound. He constructs the work on the material plane, at which level the woman stays in the background. She stands, therefore, on the right-hand side of the arcana, the 'passive side', the side of the psyche.[15]

Sometimes it is implied that while the man may experiment and labour over his retorts and materials, the woman is needed to add the right touch to bring the work to life. There is an example of this in an early Chinese text:

A gentleman of the Yellow Gate at the Han [imperial court], Cheng Wei, loved the art of the Yellow and White [alchemy]. He took a wife and secured a girl from a household which knew recipes . . . [he tried to] make gold in accordance with 'The Great Treasure' in the pillow [of the King of Huai-nan, but] it would not come. His wife however came and watched . . . Wei was then fanning the ashes to heat the bottle. In the bottle there was quicksilver. His wife said, 'I want to try and show you something.' She thereupon took a drug out of a bag and threw a very little into [the retort]. It was absorbed and in a short while she turned out [the contents of the retort]. It had already become silver. Wei was greatly astonished and said, 'The way of [alchemy] was near and was possessed by you. But why did you not tell me sooner?' His wife replied, 'In order to get it, it is necessary for one to have the [proper] fate'.[16]

Both Helvetius, whom we shall meet towards the end of this chapter, and Nicolas Flamel worked in close collaboration with their wives. In the case of Helvetius, his wife spurred him on to experiment with the powdered stone he had been given when he himself despaired of any success in the matter: 'Late that night my wife (who was a most curious student and enquirer after the art) came soliciting and vexing me to make experiment of that little spark . . . saying to me, unless this be done, I shall have no rest nor sleep all this night.' Flamel, throughout the long years of his search, was dependent upon the help and encouragement of his wife Perenelle. Together they performed the perfect alchemical transmutation, and Flamel was more than ready to acknowledge Perenelle's essential contribution: 'I may speak it with truth, I have made it three times, with the help of Perenelle, who understood it as well as I because she helped me with my operations, and without doubt, if she would have enterprised to have done it alone, she had attained the end and perfection thereof.'[17]

In all, it has to be said that alchemy was practised primarily by men, but it was not forbidden in any way to women, and it is likely that there were many women alchemists whose endeavours have passed unrecorded in history.

LABORATORIES AND THEIR INHABITANTS: MISTAKES AND DISASTERS

Contemporary paintings often show the laboratory as a busy place and one may be surprised to see a number of workers stoking, pounding, and pouring. Not all alchemists worked this way; in fact, using assistants is in some ways contrary to the spirit of alchemy, which demands secrecy and the total involvement of the practitioner rather than the delegation of work. However, the practical demands of a temperamental furnace needing to be kept at constant heat and of pots that must be watched lest they boil made the keeping of servants necessary for many. Thomas Norton decreed that eight in all would be ideal, but those of lesser fortunes might manage with four – two on duty and two that 'sleepeth or goeth to Kerke'. He also recommended that the alchemist should consult his own horoscope, especially the sixth house, to see how best to manage his servants.

The athanor (furnace) seems to have been free-standing, brick built, and about three feet in height with a conical cover on the top that could be taken off to allow a vessel to be placed in the chamber above the fire itself. Because pottery and glass vessels were needed, one of the great problems was breakages, especially at high temperatures. Thomas Charnock discusses the difficulties of ordering vessels, and of making the design explicit to the potter or the glass maker without letting him know that it is intended for alchemical use. He advises telling the potter that the wares are needed to distil water to treat blindness; making the tabernacle (or support for the vessel) needs the co-operation of a joiner, who can be told that it is a burrow for a fox!

Charnock had first-hand experience of laboratory catastrophe:

> Yet one thing of truth I weill thee tell,
> What greate mishap unto my worke befell;
> It was upon a New Yeare's Day at noon,
> My tabernacle caught fire, it was soon done:

> For within an hour it was right well,
> And straight of fire I had a smell.
> I ran up to my work right,
> And when I came it was on a fire light:
> Then was I in such fear that I began to stagger,
> As if I had been wounded to the heart with a dagger;
> And can you blame me? no I think not much,
> For if I had been a man anything rich,
> I had rather have given 100 Marks to the Poor,
> Rather than that hap should have chanced that hour.
> For I was well onward of my work truly.

Explosions and poisonings being well-known hazards of the alchemical laboratory, it is little wonder that the alchemical quest was thought of as a dangerous one, and the constant effort and devotion alchemy demanded could easily turn to obsessive mania. Bernard of Treves and Godfrey Leporis (fourteenth century), for instance, spent ten years in unsuccessful experiment, using over 2,000 hens' eggs in one project. Bernard desisted only when he was rendered unconscious by the fumes of vitriol for fourteen months. When he recovered he sold all his estate to pay his debts, and then took up alchemy again.

Some texts, such as *The Sophic Hydrolith*, give guidance so that the alchemist may judge when matters are not progressing satisfactorily. Premature redness, lack of coagulation and so on are 'symptoms of a false composition and temperature, or of some kind or other of carelessness'. The author continues: 'If these defects are not immediately seen to, they will speedily become incorrigible. A cunning adept should be acquainted with the various devices by which they may be remedied; and I will recount them here for the sake of the beginner . . .' A far worse fate is promised by an early Chinese writer should the student go astray:

Gases from food consumed will make noises inside the intestines and stomach. The right essence will be exhaled and the evil one inhaled. Days and nights will be passed without sleep, moon after moon. The body will then be tired out, giving rise to an appearance of insanity. The hundred pulses will stir and boil so violently as to drive away peace of mind and body ... Ghostly things will make their appearance, at which he will marvel even in his sleep. His is then led to rejoice, thinking that he is assured of longevity. But all of a sudden he is seized by an untimely death.[18]

It could be dangerous to let the world at large know that you practised alchemy: if people associated alchemy with the devil, they might hang you; if they thought you possessed a secret for making gold they would pursue you greedily: with kings and potentates, it was often a case of 'prove it or die'. Sometimes laws were passed forbidding the practice of alchemy, or else insisting that a special licence be obtained if the alchemist could prove himself to be a genuine seeker. The anonymous author of *An Open Entrance to the Shut Palace of the King* paints a most pathetic picture of the alchemists' lot:

So long as the secret is possessed by a comparatively small number of philosophers, their lot is anything but a bright and happy one; surrounded as we are on every side by the cruel greed and the prying suspicion of the multitude, we are doomed, like Cain, to wander over the earth homeless and friendless. Not for us are the soothing influences of domestic happiness; not for us the delightful confidences of friendship. Men who covet our golden secret pursue us from place to place, and fear closes our lips, when love tempts us to open ourselves freely to a brother. Thus we feel prompted at times to burst forth into the desolate exclamation of Cain: 'Whoever finds me will slay me.' Yet we are not the murderers of our brethren; we are anxious only to do good to our fellow-men. But even our kindness and charitable compassion are rewarded with black ingratitude – ingratitude that cries to heaven for vengeance. It was only a short time ago that, after visiting the plague-stricken haunts of a certain city, and restoring the sick to perfect health by means of my miraculous medicine, I found myself surrounded by a yelling mob, who demanded that I should give to them my Elixir of the Sages; and it was only by changing my dress and my name, by shaving off my beard

and putting on a wig, that I was enabled to save my
life . . .

LEARNING AND TEACHING

Some kindly advice to the alchemical novice is given in
the treatise as follows:

> In the first place, let him carry on his operations with
> great secrecy in order that no scornful or scurrilous person
> may know of them; for nothing discourages the beginner
> so much as the mockery, taunts and well-meant advice
> of foolish outsiders. Moreover, if he does not succeed,
> secrecy will save him from derision; if he does succeed,
> it will safeguard him against the persecution of greedy
> and cruel tyrants. In the second place, he who would
> succeed in the study of this Art should be persevering,
> industrious, learned, gentle, good-tempered, a close stu-
> dent, and neither easily discouraged nor slothful; he
> may work in co-operation with one friend, not more,
> but should be able to keep his own counsel; it is also
> necessary that he should have a little capital to procure
> the necessary implements, etc, and to provide himself
> with food and clothing while he follows this study, so
> that his mind may be undistracted by care and anxiety.
> Above all, let him be honest, God-fearing, prayerful and
> holy. Being thus equipped, he should study Nature, read
> the books of the genuine Sages, who are neither impost-
> ers nor jealous churls, and study them day and night
> . . .[19]

Many would-be alchemists tried to learn the secrets of
the art through books and manuscripts available to them.
These could produce an alternating frenzy of hope and
despair as work after work was studied and then cast
aside with the riddle still unsolved.

It was the convention in alchemical writing for each
author to slip in a hint that no work had ever been
so bold, so explicit, so ready to give away cherished
secrets.

This was usually followed by a condemnation of all
the wicked lies that had been passed off as alchemical
truths in other books:

> When I considered in my mind the great number of deceit-
> ful books and forged Alchemistic 'receipts', which have
> been put into circulation by heartless imposters, though
> they do not contain even a spark of truth — and how
> many persons have been and are still daily led astray by
> them? — it occurred to me that I could not do better than
> communicate the Talent committed to me by the Father
> of Light to the Sons and Heirs of Knowledge.[20]

Often the reader is lured on with promises of frank revelations. But time and time again this is not to be; the author
slips in an apology for not going any further, but indicates
that he has already said more than he should, 'But if
the complement is concealed let not the son of learning
wonder. For we have not concealed it from him, but have
delivered it in such a speech, as it must necessarily be hid
from the evil, and unjust, and the unwise cannot discern
it.'[21]

The message of the written texts seems to be: Let those
who understand already understand what I have written;
let those who are ignorant remain ignorant.

Although some students claimed to have mastered
alchemical practice through books, most needed a more
direct contact with the tradition. Over and over again
alchemists emphasise the fact that if the mystery is not
revealed directly through a dream or vision, then it must
come from 'living Masters'. Thomas Norton tells us that
'it must needs be taught from mouth to mouth', and that
not even one's own children are entitled to learn it. He
himself says that his master (George Ripley) tested his
sincerity in various ways, one of which was by requiring
him to ride a hundred miles in each direction to spend a
forty-day training period with his teacher. Students are
advised against wasting their money on tuition from any
vain boaster who claims to be skilled in alchemy. Only
those who know nothing, it is said, talk freely. If you are
offered instruction:

> Spend not thy money away in waste,
> Give not to every speech credence;
> But first examine, grope and taste;
> And as thou provest, so put thy confidence,

> And ever beware of great expense . . .
> One thing, one glass, one furnace and no more,
> Behold this principle if he take,
> And if he do not, then let him go . . .[22]

Some of the stories concerning the initiation of alchemists are fascinating, but even apparently factual narratives may be to some extent allegorical. Historians are generally pleased to quote the testimony of **Helvetius** (Johann Friedrich Schweitzer), for this appears to be a straighforward account of a meeting between Helvetius and an alchemical adept. The story, in brief, which is recounted in *The Golden Calf*, is that on 27 December 1666 a stranger appeared at Helvetius' house in the Hague, and showed him some pieces of matter 'each about the bigness of a small walnut, transparent, of a pale brimstone colour', which the stranger said was the Philosopher's Stone. He refused to give Helvetius any of it, but talked to him about how he could turn stones into gems, produce healing medicines, and make 'a limpid clear water sweeter than honey' (probably the famed Mercurial water). He showed Helvetius some golden medals that had been struck from alchemical gold. Three weeks later, he returned, and after much pleading from Helvetius, gave him a tiny 'crumb' of the stone. When Helvetius doubted that such a small amount could do anything at all, the stranger took it back, threw half of it into the fire, and gave him back the rest. He instructed him in the art of preparing the stone, telling him that only two substances in all are necessary, and that the work is carried out in one crucible and is neither lengthy nor expensive if correctly understood. He did not return again, but Helvetius, with the assistance of his wife, performed a successful transmutation with the stone, and the gold which was produced was publicly assayed and found to be of excellent quality.

Some scholars have found this story difficult to assess, for on the one hand Helvetius was a respected physician and botanical writer, not given to deliberate deception; yet on the other, the tale of marvellous gold produced in this way seems to them to have little credibility. I would suggest that much of the tale is likely to be allegory.

A clever man such as Helvetius is quite capable of weaving his knowledge of alchemical training into a kind of parable, which contains much information and truth but not in a literal fashion. Indeed, it is much more likely that he would do this than that he would openly describe his training, since it was normal for this to be kept secret.

The stranger who mysteriously arrives is described as wearing 'a plebeian habit, honest Gravity, and serious authority; of a mean stature, a little long face, with a few small pock holes, and most black hair, not at all curled, a beardless chin, about three or four and forty years of age (as I guessed)'. Such a description is a perfect portrait of Saturn personified. The astrological attributes of Saturn (as we have seen, alchemists were well-versed in planetary lore) when applied to human appearance are leanness, dark hair and complexion, a lowliness of clothing and height, and a serious manner. Saturn, additionally was sometimes depicted as the wise guide and instructor in alchemy, who could lead the initiate to understanding. Even the anecdotal detail that the stranger forgot to wipe the snow and mud off his boots when entering Helvetius' nicely-furnished room has a significance in this context, for Saturn is the planet of dirt and earth, and those under his influence are said to be somewhat grubby in their own manners and appearance.

And what of Helvetius himself, as he portrays his reactions? His behaviour is just like that of Mercury, the agent of alchemy — ever-questioning, arguing, even trying to steal the Stone at one point. Mercury is the natural active force of alchemy; in its primal state it is volatile and unreliable and must be disturbed, released and then fixed in a higher state in order to bring about the transformation.

5 · A MIRROR OF THE WORLD

It may be asked whether such a secretive, enigmatic study as alchemy has any relevance at all to the world at large. How could it possibly benefit humanity, or add to our general store of knowledge, especially when its adherents make a virtue out of keeping its inner teachings strictly to themselves? One can argue, however, that any philosophy, religious movement or esoteric study, can serve as a ground plan for human endeavour if it there is truth at its heart. If its structure is rooted in universal principles, in what is sometimes referred to as 'the perennial philosophy', then it can affect every level of human existence, right through from the spiritual to the practical. Even if its inner teachings remain concealed, perhaps for a number of years, perhaps permanently, it will almost inevitably affect the course of human endeavour sooner or later. Esoteric becomes exoteric; theory turns into practice; abstract becomes concrete. It can be said that the capacity of a wisdom tradition to bear fruit in everyday life is at least as important as the illumination of its followers.

In the case of alchemy, its influence can be traced in scientific discoveries, in literature and the arts, and in the development of modern psychology. Sometimes these developments were brought about by those who were themselves deeply involved in the study of alchemy; sometimes they were the result of borrowings from the alchemical framework and language. Some discoveries, particularly in the scientific field, were by-products of working on the alchemical process, whereas other applications of alchemy were fuelled by taking the essence of its philosophy and symbolism and creating afresh.

In this chapter and the two that follow, we shall be looking at ways in which alchemy served as inspiration in different contexts. In certain cases the link is very direct, in others it may be speculative, or be tied in to other occult and philosophical traditions. Points at which such traditions, especially ones as secretive as alchemy, cross the threshold into the outer world, are not always easy to spot. Disovering such points, however, can be tremendously exciting, reconnecting us with the energy of the original inspiration, and broadening and enlivening our vision of the subject concerned. Perhaps it is not too fanciful to say that it is the completion of the creative process: the spiritual impulse works its way through to a material form; the impulse is forgotten; then, when it is rediscovered, by people from a different time and place, it rebinds itself to the divine creative force ('religion' – to rebind) making a new link between the temporal and the eternal. This in its turn can lead to further creation, just as the reconnection with the philosophy of the ancient masters Plato and Aristotle, and with the hermetic texts, helped to inspire the European Renaissance – the word Renaissance itself means rebirth.

Inevitably, as knowledge is brought into the general realm, it can become dissipated, and even undermine existing spiritual traditions. Isaac Newton, as we shall see in the following chapter, was both a passionate mystic and an alchemical adept, and yet his scientific discoveries led to a school of scientific thought that rejected anything that could not be weighed, measured or quantified. Dion Fortune, an occult writer associated with the Golden Dawn (see Chapter 8) and other esoteric orders, remarked darkly that techniques commonly used by advertising agencies were once only known to initiates of such orders. In this case, one may surmise that such techniques, probably involving the power of image and suggestion, may not only have become popularised but have also been applied to very dubious ends. Such examples make more sense of the anxiety of the alchemists to keep their knowledge hidden, lest it should fall into the wrong hands.

ALCHEMY AND BAROQUE MUSIC

This exploration begins, as the Lady Alchymia steps out shyly into the sunlight, with a look at the link between alchemy and the birth of baroque music. These two subjects have rarely been linked, and yet there is a powerful connection between the them. The greatest composer of the time, Claudio Monteverdi, was a practising alchemist, and other leading composers of the day were dedicated to tapping sources of ancient wisdom and channelling it into their work; studies of this kind prevalent in northern Italy at the time included alchemy, Neoplatonism, astrology, and the Cabbala.

Baroque music, as this 'new music' came to be known, arose in the years between 1570 and 1610. Its effect was remarkable, for in that brief period, music was revolutionised. New forms of solo singing and instrumental music were created; music and drama found a true fusion, and from their union sprang opera and oratorio. Its innovation heralded a musical era which lasted for nearly two hundred years, and whose composers included such great names as Bach, Handel, Purcell and Vivaldi. Many of its forms and idioms have remained in musical currency until the present day, and of course Baroque music itself is alive and well on the concert platform. In fact it seems that the music is appreciated more than ever before – there is a growing love of its clarity and beauty, of music which is structured as graciously as fine architecture, yet is also full of vitality and power.

When we start digging down to discover the connections between alchemy and Baroque music, we come across different kinds of evidence. There are direct links: Monteverdi's recorded interest in alchemy, and his avowed intent to weave philosophical truths into his music. There are inferences to be made: from the fact that alchemical practice was widespread in northern Italy at the time, and that the groups of learned men and composers working to create a new form of music would have almost certainly included it among their mystical and metaphysical studies. Finally, there are the parallels which we ourselves can spot between the practice of alchemy and Baroque music, all leading to a greater understanding of the creative process at work behind the compositions.

We are just at the beginning of this fascinating exploration, and I think it likely that more and more evidence connecting the two subjects will be brought to light in future years. In later chapters I offer you examples of other links already researched between alchemy and the arts and sciences; in this chapter I present my own area of investigation, which has captured my attention both as a singer specialising in this period of music, and as a writer focusing on 'magical philosophies' such as alchemy.

MONTEVERDI, ALCHEMY AND THE FLORENTINE CAMERATA

There was a strong tradition of alchemical study in northern Italy, which was composed geographically of various independent ducal states. Many dukes and nobles showed a keen interest in alchemy, in a climate of learning that was favourable to occult traditions set in a framework of studies which covered a wide spectrum of arts and natural sciences. Often the traces of alchemical study remain in the buildings themselves. A room was set aside in the Uffizi Palace in Florence for the study of alchemy, and apparently the 'studiolo' or small study in the Palazzo Vecchio, also in Florence, was dedicated to the same purpose. Both these would have been used in the sixteenth century. Dating from an earlier period, alchemical paintings can be found in the Palazzo del Popolo in San Gimignano, near Siena. These frescoes are thought to have been painted by Memmo di Filipuccio between 1303 and 1317. Those that survive cover a large part of the walls of a small upper room in the tower (one of the famous medieval 'skyscraper' towers of the city) and depict themes such as the wedding and bedding of the alchemical King and Queen, the immersion of the royal pair in the bath, and the flagellation of the man/animal representing the First Substance. A six-petalled golden flower, symbolising the alchemical goal, is repeated as a motif over the frescoes, and a mysterious lady, probably the Lady Alchymia herself, as the spirit of alchemy was often represented, acts as guide and initiator into each new pictorial sequence. Strangely enough, these have not yet been recognised by scholars as alchemical, although near exact illustrative parallels can be found in many alchemical sources; one guidebook assumes that they represent 'an evident moralizing intention . . . showing what dangers one can meet with in succumbing to female seduction.'

Returning to the sixteenth century, Vincenzo Gonzaga, the Duke of Mantua, and Monteverdi's first patron, was a keen student of alchemy. It is thought that this is where the young composer was initiated into the art. Monteverdi's own practice of alchemy lasted a lifetime, and a sonnet written in his praise shortly after his death described him as a 'Great Master of Alchemy'. There are various mentions of alchemy in Monteverdi's letters, although he is, in the best tradition, cryptic in his references. He describes and draws a vessel for calcinating gold with lead, and speaks of his own experiments in making mercury from 'unrefined matter which changes into clear water' which, 'although it will be in water it will not however lose its identity as mercury, or its weight.' In later letters he conceals the nature of substances he is referring to, speaking only of 'a pot of it', 'a small jar of it' and 'a certain something'.

These letters were written during Monteverdi's later years when he worked as master of music at St Mark's Basilica, Venice, a place where he composed some of his finest works, such as the Vespers of 1610. The editor of his letters refers to Gonzaga's interest in alchemy as 'an unhealthy enthusiasm for the pseudo-sciences' and suggests that Monteverdi's own involvement 'could not have been all that deep'.[1] And yet Monteverdi, it is widely accepted, was ardently involved with the quest for wisdom, a follower of Plato actively endeavouring to centre his music around those truths. 'My intention is to show by means of our practice (i.e. musical practice, his 'Seconda Pratica') what I have been able to extract from the mind of those philosophers for the benefit of good art'. We shall meet some of those means later. For the moment, it is enough to recognise that alchemy, a subject in which Monteverdi took a great interest, and for which he became famous as an adept in his own time, would have influenced his musical composition just as the classical philosophers did.

It is also worth knowing that music was considered an intrinsic part of alchemy by many alchemists of the period. Sometimes the Great Work was conducted with the assistance of musical chants. Illustrations contemporary with the beginnings of Baroque music such as those contained in *Splendor Solis*, by Trismosin (c. 1582) and *The Amphitheatre of Eternal Wisdom*, by Heinrich Kunrath (1609) show musical instruments in the laboratory, or groups of players and singers as emblematic of stages in the alchemical process. Thus music could be a magical aid in the laboratory, invoking, perhaps, planetary spirits; it was also a guide to cosmic laws in which the power of vibration, sound, and mathematical ratios may be understood.

An even more fascinating and direct use of music in alchemy is found in Michael Maier's *Emblems, Fugues and Epigrams* (1617), now available in a new 'performing' edition (Translated and edited by Joscelyn Godwin, with accompanying cassette recording, Phanes Press 1989). Here Maier sets fifty vocal fugues for three voices as musical illustrations for the beautifully drawn alchemical emblems, many of which are well known in their own right. They are more than illustrations: they are, Maier says, 'for the soul's recreation ... to be looked at, read, meditated, understood, weighed, sung and listened to, not without a certain pleasure.' Music and alchemy had already found their fusion in the alchemical laboratory; while Maier cultivated this connection within the hermetic sphere, composers such as Monteverdi took it out into the wider cultural field.

Monteverdi was an individualist; although he took note of progress made by other composers in the field, he felt that he had to work out his own salvation, with the help of such traditions as Neoplatonism and alchemy. However, the earliest developments of Baroque music in the late sixteenth century were inspired by collective study. The group responsible is generally known as 'the Florentine Camerata', an active fraternity of musicians, scholars and nobles, whose avowed aim was to restore music to the glory of ancient classical civilisation, with the help not only of the philosophers of the time but of a whole range of metaphysical, mystical and magical studies, in which alchemy would have found a natural place. The key figure in organising the groups which met was Giovanni Bardi, whose son later wrote:

> My father, Signor Giovanni, who took great delight in music and was in his day a composer of some reputation, always had about him the most celebrated men of the city, learned in this profession, and inviting them to his house, he formed a sort of delightful and continual academy, from which vice and in particular every kind of gaming were absent. To this the noble youth of Florence were attracted with great profit to themselves, passing their time not only in pursuit of music, but also in discussing and receiving instruction in poetry, astrology and other sciences which by turns lent value to this pleasant converse.[2]

The Florentine Camerata was an academy (in fact it probably consisted of two or three consecutive groups) following a tradition established in Florence in 1459 by Marsilio Ficino. Ficino responded to a request from the reigning duke, Cosimo di Medici, to found a new school of study based on the rediscovered writings of Plato and the Hermetic texts (see p. 92). Here, studies in Cabbala and astrology interwove with these classical and hermetic themes, and its members endeavoured to show that there was no fundamental clash between such teachings and Christianity. This original Florentine Academy had a profound effect upon the religious and artistic outlook of the time. It was succeeded by a number of other academies, each with a slightly different outlook or intention.

The Florentine Camerata, over one hundred years later, maintained this broad outlook, but applied it to specific musical goals. Its output was at first rather pedantic; making music by committee resulted, not unsurprisingly, in somewhat contrived compositions. However, certain principles that its members laid down began to bear fruit; the declamatory style (later known as recitative) was devised from their interpretation of Greek drama, giving a means of turning the passionate expression of speech into music. Soon true individual creativity started to reveal itself with composers such as Giulio Caccini and Jacopo Peri whose work has proved itself to be of lasting value. In keeping with the traditions of wisdom they turned to for inspiration, their goals were spiritual ones: Caccini wrote that the aim of music was that it should appear to be 'a pattern and true resemblance of those never ceasing celestial harmonies whence proceed so many good effects and benefits upon earth, raising and exciting the minds of the hearers to the contemplation of those infinite delights which Heaven affordeth.'[3]

In general terms, such aims parallelled those of alchemy. As with alchemical practice, members of the Camerata also believed that humans can actively participate in the creative process in the universe, that we are not passive onlookers but can weave our own magic, and invoke presences of gods and angels. The gods, it was said, can be affected by our music. Antecedents for this are found in the writings of Ficino who recommended using music as a means to call down the planetary deities. (*Giordano Bruno and the Hermetic Tradition* – Frances Yates p. 77–8) This is turn derives from Orphic practices, which are linked in time and context with the hermetic writings (see p. 92), bringing us back full circle to alchemy. The prevalent hermetic interest in Italy in the Renaissance can also be judged from the marble pavement in the Cathedral in Siena, where striking portraits of Hermes Trismegistus and the ten prophetic Sibyls can be seen.

NATURE AND MUSIC

Let Nature be your guide, and with your art
Follow her closely. Without her you'll err.
Let reason be your staff; experience lend
Power to your sight, that you may see afar.
Let reading be your lamp, dispelling dark,
That you may guard 'gainst throngs of things and words.
       (Epigram 42 – Michael Maier – Atlanta Fugiens)

Let us turn now to examine more specific alchemical ideas as they appear in Baroque music. Some may be culled directly from the alchemical tradition, whereas it is only fair to say that others may have been derived from a synthesis of alchemy, astrology, cabbalism and Neoplatonism. There are in any case many parallels and overlaps between those traditions, which constantly borrowed one from the other. We are standing on one of those elusive thresholds, the point at which esoteric becomes exoteric, tentatively remaking that connection so that our understanding and appreciation of music can be re-energised.

First of all, alchemy and Baroque music emphasise the role of Nature, as a guiding principle, as a teacher whose ways were to be understood, imitated, and transformed through art. The word 'natural' occurs time and time again in the writings of the Florentine Camerata. The members felt that artifice had taken the place of a natural approach to music. They aimed to create a music that would sound natural and spontaneous and yet be of great subtlety, with the power to move the listener and evoke the 'heavenly harmonies' within an earthly framework. The human voice was their touchstone of the natural and instinctive, the 'Primal Material' of musical alchemy. In practical terms this resulted in an emphasis on a solo voice, where words and expression might be properly communicated, on the avoidance of extremes in pitch and dynamic – the singer, said Caccini, should 'so pitch his tune as to sing in his clear and natural voice' – and the addition of ornaments only where they served to grace the music, rather than to show off the performer's expertise.

A quotation from the famous illuminated alchemical manuscript *Splendor Solis* echoes this approach:

Fig. 6 'For him versed in Chemistry, let Nature, Reason, Experience, and Reading be his Guide, staff, spectacles and lamp.' (From Atlanta Fugiens by Michael Maier.)

Art goes quite another way to work, with different intention from Nature, therefore does Art also use different tools and instruments. For that reason can Art produce extraordinary things out of the aforesaid natural beginnings such as Nature of herself would not be able to create.[4]

Monteverdi also pays tribute to the importance of seeking out the natural and transforming it into music of great power and refinement. Like the alchemists, he believed in searching the wisdom of the ancient masters for clues but then working out one's own solution. In a letter written in 1633, Monteverdi says that he sought 'a natural way of imitation', but that when he was composing his Lament of Arianna (one of his most famous and profound pieces) 'no book could show me ... not even one that would explain how I ought to become

77

an imitator . . . I found out (let me tell you) what hard work I had to do in order to achieve the little I did do in the way of imitation.' However, in a subsequent letter written in February 1634, he acknowleges that he had found a certain guidance from 'the principles of the best philosophers to have investigated nature'.[5]

Searching the ancient wisdom, the forgotten knowledge and despised material, working intensively from one's own observations, often until near breaking point, was the way in which both the alchemist and the Baroque composer struggled to release the potent forces of Nature and begin the process of creation. In his account of the Florentine Camerata, Pietro de' Bardi recalls how his father, in collaboration with Vincenzo Galilei, a founding member and father of the famous astronomer Galileo Galilei, dedicated himself to the quest:

> This great intellect [Galilei] recognised that, besides restoring ancient music . . . one of the chief aims of the academy was to improve modern music . . . Thus he was the first to let us hear singing in *stile rappresentativo*, in which arduous undertaking, then considered almost ridiculous, he was chiefly encouraged and assisted by my father, who toiled for entire nights and incurred great expense for the sake of this noble discovery.[6]

The composers who 'invented' Baroque music – the Florentine Camerata, Monteverdi and his contemporaries – did not simply feel a song coming on and write it down. Like the alchemists, they worked with conscious intent, using a combination of the ancient wisdom, personal repeated effort, observation and individual vision to achieve the transformation.

BATTLING DUOS, HARMONIOUS TRIOS

The next parallel between music and alchemy can be found in the generation of warring opposites. One of the radical innovations in Baroque music was that it deliberately employed the use of sharp successive contrasts, to increase tension and heighten the drama of a piece. Often these contrasts are quite violent, and occur within a very short musical space, so that, for instance, within a sacred choral piece one may hear the voices join in a few bars of smooth polyphony, and then break into an urgent, agitated passage. At the time this must have been almost shocking, but very exciting. In alchemy, early in the process, the First Matter is violently split into two to release the dynamic polarities within. The stage is often described as a battle, a duel between a pair of men, dogs or dragons. This energy can then be used to fuel the alchemical transformation; in order to arrive at final resolution and transformation, conflict must be provoked. 'I was aware that it is contraries that greatly move our mind, and . . . this is the purpose which all good music should have' Monteverdi wrote, as he described his search to find a form of music fitting to represent warfare – a search to which he 'applied [himself] with no small diligence and toil'.[7]

This leads to our next correspondence, moving from the concept of a basic duality to that of the three forces which may be seen to underpin both the alchemical process and a musical structure. In music they correspond to three 'modes' of expression; in alchemy they are salt, mercury and sulphur, or body, soul and spirit. This fundamental triplicity is not exclusive to alchemy, and is found with different names in the Cabbala, in Platonic philosophy and of course in the Christian doctrine of the Trinity. However, actively working with the triplicity, rather than just acknowledging it, is especially emphasised in alchemy, and this process of engaging with the three forces may, I believe, give us insight into the interpretation of Baroque music.

It was Monteverdi who innovated and established this principle of a threefold means of expression in music.

I have reflected that the principal passions or affections of our mind are three, namely, anger, moderation, and humility or supplication; so the best philosophers declare, and the very nature of our voice indicates this in having high, low and middle registers. The art of music also points to these three in its terms 'agitated', 'soft' and 'moderate' (concitato, molle, and temperato). In all the works of former composers I have indeed found examples of the 'soft' and the 'moderate', but never of the 'agitated'.[8]

Thus Monteverdi began work on creating a means of musically representing warfare, as mentioned above. Basically, the style he evolved, known as 'concitato', consists of rapidly reiterated ated notes which are centred on a regular pulse but adapted to the rhythm and sense of the words being sung.

It is possible that this dynamic working trinity may underlie musical composition of the time to a greater extent than has hitherto been realised. With his Platonic and alchemical training, Monteverdi would have seen the triplicity not simply as a trio of emotions demanding expression, but as a way of describing the fundamental three forces of creation in human terms. Michael Maier, in his alchemical fugues, did just that, using the classical myth of Atlanta, the swift-footed virgin, and personifying mercury, sulphur and salt as Atlanta, Hippomenes and the Golden Apple respectively. Here the three voices sing concurrently; their parts are structured to symbolise their individual natures, and the harmonies and musical progressions symbolise the changing interaction between them. Both Maier's own preface to the work and editorial analysis leave no doubt that he intended to paint as dynamic a musical portrait of the alchemical triplicity as possible, turning the philosophic mercury, the fiery sulphur and the quiet, steady salt into living music.

So far, we have seen that the three creative forces of alchemy can be musically structured both in terms of harmony and also as stylistic modes of expression. It is also possible that they may have been used to provide a sectional groundplan for music, in which each part of the triplicity is highlighted in turn. If we look at certain compositions in this light, new avenues of interpretation open up. Take, for example, the *Lamento d'Arianna*, written in 1608. This is an extended solo lament; it was the climactic piece of a complete opera by Monteverdi based on the myth of Ariadne and Theseus, considered a masterpiece in its day but now unfortunately lost in its entirety. The lament is a complex succession of emotions as Ariadne faces her abandonment, and her mixed passions of love and anger for Theseus. However, if we consider it as falling into three sections, immediately the predominating mood of each reveals itself in accord with the 'molle', the 'concitato' and the 'moderato.' In the first section, Ariadne alternately begs for death and for Theseus to return to her; it is the 'molle', the soft, beseeching, loving force. In the second, her resentment and anger takes over; she invokes tempests and whirlwinds to destroy Theseus on his journey home. Here, plainly, is the 'concitato' style, both in theme and in musical notation. Finally, she enters the state of 'moderato'; her grief is still present, but she becomes reconciled with dignity to her fate, and takes farewell of her parents and her homeland. Her fate, she says, is of one who has loved and trusted too much.

If we use this triplicity as a guide to this marvellous, difficult and lengthy piece, it provides a revelation of interpretation, a guide to the singer and listener. It also structures the lament like a complete miniature tragedy in its own right (it was considered to be such at the time) ending, through the moderato mode, with a kind of ultimate resolution and reconciliation.

THE COSMIC STAGE

The audience watching a Baroque opera is like an alchemist gazing into his vessel. The changing fortunes of kings and queens, intimate visions of the gods and the interaction of heaven and earth are dramas which are witnessed by both. Just as the alchemist saw his vessel as a miniature cosmos, so the Baroque stage was a complete world; it was even set out so that one part represented heaven and another earth. Certain stage plays of the period also exhibit alchemical overtones, and in Chapter 7 we can look more closely at these. Opera, however, was more cosmological; gods, angels, spirits and figures from allegories move among mortals in a way that is rarer in plays and there is a more obvious sense of magical evocation. Its music, as with Ficino's hymns, is used as a means to create communion between earthly and heavenly forces.

Opera was thus not merely a performance; by putting drama into music one was actually calling forth the spirit of the gods and that of the myth, which was usually taken from classical sources. Both opera and alchemy were seen as active, participatory processes – alchemy too used classical mythology at this time to describe the different stages of the work. In opera, music was the means to awaken the myth, and all – composer, performers and audience – were participants in the process.

Curiously enough, this notion of participation is expressed very plainly in the English masque form. Masques were glorious costumed displays of music, song and dance, given with dazzling effects of colour and lighting. Plots were thin or non-existent, but there was great emphasis on representing different levels of creation, so that angels and apes might take the stage together. Masques were almost always performed by and given before the nobility, ideally with the king and queen present. The cosmos was revealed, with the alchemical king and queen as witnesses. Then, at the end of the masque, the audience was obliged to get up and join in the dancing, with the king and queen, or highest ranking couple there, leading the festivities. There is no proof as yet that alchemy was a direct inspiration for this, but I think that alchemy explains very well just why the form of the masque should be structured this way.

In this chapter we have opened out the enclosed, secretive world of alchemy and looked at its influence on Baroque music. By doing this, a door opens; more and more possibilities present themselves, and one begins to see that our understanding of music of the time could be profoundly affected by this knowledge. I would like to think that by understanding the relationship between alchemy and music, both factual and conceptual, we may find inspiration powerful enough to affect the course of future music composition and performance. It is more than a new light on old music; it could be the key to releasing new creativity and to transforming the present musical structures by which composers, performers and audiences are bound. Alchemy and music of the sixteenth and seventeenth centuries both had the same aim: 'Hermes, a Father of Philosophy, says: "It is indeed needed that at the End of this World, Heaven and Earth should meet and come home"'.(*Splendor Solis*).

6 · ALCHEMY AS A SPIRITUAL DISCIPLINE

The greedy cheat with impure hands may not
Attempt this Art, nor is it ever got
By the unlearned and rude: the vicious mind
To lust and softness given, it strikes stark blind,
So the sly wandering factor . . .
But the sage, pious man, who still adores
And loves his Maker, and his love implores,
Whoever joys to search the secret cause
And series of his works, their love and laws,
Let him draw near, and joining will with strength,
Study this Art in all her depth and length;
Then grave experience shall his consort be
Skilled in large nature's inmost mystery.
The knots and doubts his busy course and cares
Will oft disturb, till time the truth declares,
And stable patience, through all trials passed,
Brings the glad end and long hoped for, at last.[1]

The alchemical operation works on three levels of
being at once – on body, soul and spirit. The hermetic
philosophy maintains that everything – animal, vegetable and mineral – contains these three elements, but
in an unawakened form. The Great Work breaks down
the existing relationship between them, activating each

separately, and leading them from an ignorant and inert state to perfection. The alchemist initiates this operation both in the materials he works with in his laboratory and in his own being. He aims to free the soul and spirit of matter and to reunite them with the body in a new and exalted form; he also attempts this task in his own life. Prayer, observation and work are the tools he uses to activate his own spiritual, psychological and physical faculties.

Although all mainstream alchemy embodies this triple approach in principle, yet different schools and adepts have often chosen to emphasise one aspect in particular, and this engenders different qualities in the type of alchemy that results. Broadly speaking, alchemy emphasising the perfection of the body usually dwells more on metals and materials, the laboratory processes, and tangible results. This line of alchemy is the one most likely to give rise to chemical and scientific discoveries. Alchemy that gives the soul special consideration is likely to concern itself primarily with medicinal results and to seek for curative and healing agents – the art of the Elixir. It may use more vegetable than metallic matter in its work of preparation. Alchemy of the spirit put the greatest efforts into the illumination of man himself, and may regard the physical and tangible results of alchemy as secondary. It lays emphasis on the role of contemplation within the alchemical work and tends to draw in religious and philosophical teaching. The effects of alchemy of body and soul will be considered in the next chapter; alchemy of the spirit will be the prime focus of this one.

ALCHEMY AS SPIRITUAL DEVELOPMENT

To set the picture for a discussion of specific examples of spiritual alchemy, I shall give some indication of how the alchemical process works at a parallel level in the alchemist himself.

The Primal Material that the alchemical seeker takes to work on at the spiritual level is himself. He is made in the image of God and contains the seeds of soul and spirit within him. These are, to some extent, imprisoned in the body; in order to release them that they may grow to perfection he must summon up the will and intention to start the work and make the initial effort to dissolve this apparent unity. The body is not rejected as such, but it must be encouraged to loosen its hold upon the inner being so that the process of transformation can begin. This can be set in motion by embracing the alchemical discipline itself; the student decides to commit himself to a task that will demand the utmost in patience and concentration. His old way of life will be disrupted, since most of his resources – money, time and mental effort – will be channelled into the alchemical work. There is no immediate gratification in terms of quick results, and no guarantee of success at all. Nor is there any turning back; the process both in the laboratory and in the human soul is considered irreversible. Although, in hermetic understanding, all first matter grows to gold in due course, and man himself evolves towards greater consciousness as part of a natural process, yet the change is usually too slow for individuals to perceive and experience: alchemy seeks to accelerate this change and bring about the possibility of completion within a personal life-span.

The labours of the alchemical work activate the faculties of the seeker, and the frustrations experienced in trying to find the right materials and correct sequence of operation will keep him alert and observant. The alchemists relate that when the initial dissolution has taken place, the Mercurial water can be extracted and reserved for future use. This 'water' corresponds to the elements of hope and faith the aspirant discovers within himself. All men and women have some intimation or experience of the divine in their lives, but sometimes this is locked away or rendered impotent by doubt. The first stage of dissolution allows a person to see this 'treasure' for what it really is. It should then be 'stored away' safely ready for later use, rather than subjected to the upheavals and even violence of the subsequent stages. Then, when there is resolution of the conflict (corresponding to the stage where the 'child' is born in the vessel), it can be added or released to nurture the growing creation with hope and love.

After the alchemical material has been prepared and

put through the initial stages of dissolution and activation, it is heated in the sealed vessel. The sealed vessel corresponds to the secrecy with which the work is carried out, an important ingredient of spiritual discipline. The aspirant must be willing to keep his own counsel, confiding only in his teacher, if he has one – otherwise all is lost through evaporation or dissipation. (This is similar to the creative process in the arts, where it is advisable for the writer, musician or painter not to subject the work in progress to outside opinion until it is fully 'born', to prevent the inspiration and energy from disappearing completely.)

What is the heat that is applied to the vessel? In one sense, it is the student's aim, kept always to the fore, like a fire burning within. This corresponds to the 'burning love' of the mystics, without which they would lose heart and lack the courage to face the difficulties they encounter. In another way it can correspond to the friction caused by demanding tasks in the laboratory that stretch him to his limits of endurance. However, in alchemy it is stated that the heat must be carefully regulated otherwise the vessel may crack and break: the energies the alchemist expends on laboratory work, research and religious prayer must all be tempered or else a harmful frenzy or mania can result.

In the apparatus, the liquid is circulated over and over again, being distilled and redistilled to a degree that most scientists would consider pointless. The alchemists maintain that this is the only way to further the transformation of the material. If the action is performed with patience, attention and care, it will have results on the psychological level too. It is similar to certain religious and meditational practices, such as the orthodox Christian discipline of the 'prayer of the heart', which consists of repeating silently a short and simple prayer over and over again until it becomes a ceaseless and perpetual activity. Such repetitive practices are far from meaningless if carried out correctly, releasing potent and vital energies that will help to fuel the transformation.

This concept is made explicit in a Chinese book, *The Secret of the Golden Flower*, an alchemical-mystical text dating from around the eighth or ninth century AD. The work contains instructions for meditation based on the 'circulation of the light' within until it crystallizes into the Elixir:

> The Golden Flower is the light. What colour is the light? One uses the Golden Flower as a symbol. It is the true energy of the transcendent great One . . . When the light circulates, the energies of the whole body appear before its throne, as, when a holy king has established the capital and has laid down the fundamental rules of order, all the states approach with tribute . . . Therefore you have only to make the light circulate: that is the deepest and most wonderful secret. The light is easy to move, but difficult to fix. If it is made to circulate long enough, then it crystallizes itself; that is the natural spirit body . . . The Golden Flower is the Elixir of Life.[2]

From its earliest recorded history, alchemy has contained all the ingredients necessary for a discipline that is to be practised within one's own being as well as in the laboratory retort. The process is described in terms of living beings – of dragons, fishes, birds, and of human archetypes, such as the king and queen, images which speak to us of our own elemental nature. The identification of the alchemist with his work is the chief distinction between alchemy and science, for while the scientist attempts to stand outside the experiment in order to obtain 'objective' results, the alchemist only values results that are obtained by personal effort and involvement.

Even the four elements of earth, water, fire and air must be brought into the correct balance in the personal realm; special attention is paid to the mastery of fire and water, for these two elements are contrary to one another in their action and are mutually destructive. The reconciliation of fire and water was a central aim in the process of perfection: 'The things that are in the realms above are also in the realms beneath; what heaven shows is often found on earth. Fire and flowing water are contrary to one another; Happy thou, if thou canst unite them: let it suffice thee to know this!'[3] This process was often symbolized by the seal of Solomon, the double triangle interlaced with one apex pointing upwards and one down, representing the uniting of the heavenly and earthly principles.

The 'spiritual alchemists' frequently made much use of the doctrine of the three principles – Mercury, Salt and Sulphur. In most alchemical texts it becomes obvious that Mercury, as the soul, is the chief agent in alchemy, mediating between body and spirit and performing the transformations at each stage. Salt, the body, must perish and be resurrected, and Sulphur, the spirit, must soar like the eagle and attain to knowledge.

> When he [Sulphur] is set free, he binds his gaolers, and gives their three kingdoms to his deliverer. He also gives to him a magic mirror, in which the three parts of the wisdom of the whole world may be seen and known at a glance: and this mirror clearly exhibits the creation of the world, the influences of the celestial virtues of earthly things, and the way in which Nature composed substances by the regulation of heat.[4]

The texts show over and over again that knowledge and wisdom were devoutly sought by the alchemists: Sendivogius calls the alchemists 'the children of knowledge'. Sometimes the Great Work is illustrated in pictorial form as a mountain up which the seeker must climb, encountering dangers and trials at every turn of the path. The alchemist was often exhorted to search for the Primal Matter on the summit of a mountain:

> On the other side of the fourth leaf, he painted a fair flower on the top of a very high mountain, which was sore shaken with the north wind: it had the foot blue, the flowers white and red, the leaves shining like fine gold, and round about it the dragons and griffons of the North made their nests and abode . . .[5]

ALCHEMY AND CHRISTIANITY

In Europe, the tradition of spiritual alchemy became strongly identified with Christianity, and the alchemical operation was explained as the mystical path through which the individual could become one with Christ, who is himself the perfect Stone. The earliest source that draws the parallel between alchemy and Christianity is identified by C. G. Jung as the *Margarita Pretiosa*, written by Petrus Bonus of Ferrar in the fourteenth century. By the sixteenth and seventeenth centuries this approach had become well established, and authors exercised their metaphysical ingenuity in drawing correspondences between Christian and alchemical teaching.

In *The Sophic Hydrolith* the life of Jesus is equated with the transformation of the Stone in the alchemical process. The fire that heats the material is like the 'furnace of affliction' that Jesus had to pass through when he was rejected and insulted by men. The period of 'chemical digestion', the forty-day gestation period of the seed in the vessel, is like the forty-day-and-night fast that Christ spent in the wilderness. And the life of Christ has given us the elements we need for personal redemption, for his baptism and crucifixion are the water and spirit that will regenerate us when we have ourselves passed through the furnace and come to the 'true black Raven's head', the mortification when beauty and reputation are lost and intense suffering is experienced. This particular text shows that alchemy can be a truly spiritual and Christian discipline, whilst retaining a concern with practical alchemy; other writers, however, began to pay less attention to the laboratory aspects of the work and taught alchemy purely as a devotional and mystical discipline.

The most famous of these is **Jacob Boehme** (1575–1624), whose writings are highly complex and enigmatic, containing descriptions of man's relationships to God and Christ couched in alchemical terms. Boehme's knowledge of alchemy was profound, but he began life as an untutored shoemaker having little concern for religious matters. The story of his conversion is related as follows:

> One day while tending his master's shoe shop, a mysterious stranger entered who, while he seemed to possess but little of this world's goods, appeared to be most wise and noble in spiritual attainment. The stranger asked the price of a pair of shoes, but young Boehme did not dare to name a figure, for fear that he would displease his master. The stranger insisted and Boehme finally placed a

valuation which he felt was all that his master possibly could hope to secure for the shoes. The stranger
immediately bought them and departed. A short distance
down the street the mysterious stranger stopped and cried
out in a loud voice, 'Jakob, Jakob, come forth'. In amaze-
ment and fright, Boehme ran out of the house. The strange
man fixed his eyes upon the youth – great eyes which
sparkled and seemed filled with divine light. He took the
boy's right hand and addressed him as follows: 'Jakob,
thou art little, but shalt be great, and become another man,
such a one as at whom the world shall wonder.[6]

Boehme saw that the conflict induced between the
warring elements in the alchemical vessel was an emblem of the activity of nature itself. Without conflict
there could be no movement, no difference between
created beings, and no motivation to bring about change
and improvement.

This essential combat is to be cured finally by 'the light
of nature' and by 'the desire of the spirit'. Boehme's sum-
mary of the alchemical spiritual work is as follows:

[Man] lies now shut up after his fall in a gross, de-
formed, bestial dead image; he is not like an angel,
much less like unto paradise; he is as the gross ore
in Saturn, wherein the gold is couched and shut up;
his paradisical image is in him as if it were not, and
it is also not manifest, the outward body is a stinking
carcass, while it yet lives in the poison; he is a bad thorny
bush, from whence notwithstanding fair rose-buds may
bloom forth, and grow out of the thorns, and manifest
that which lies hidden, and shut up in the wrathful
poisonful Mercury, till the artist who has made him
takes him in hand, and brings the living Mercury into
his gold or paradisical image disappeared and shut up in
death; so that the inclosed image, which was created out
of the divine meekness and love-essentiality, may again
bud and spring forth in the divine Mercury, viz. in the
word of the Deity, which entered in the humanity shut
up . . .

And then the divine Mercury changes the wrathful
Mercury into its property, and Christ is born, who
bruises the head of the serpent . . . and a new man

arises in holiness and righteousness, which lives before God, [and his divine image] appears and puts forth its lustre as the hidden gold out of the earthly property.[7]

Boehme's injection of alchemy into Christianity inspired many of the mystics and thinkers who succeeded him.

Two other writers of the seventeenth century famous for their interest in alchemy are Henry and Thomas Vaughan. The Vaughans were twins, born in Breconshire in 1621, and both studied at Oxford. Thomas, the lesser known of the two, had a colourful career as a doctor, as a priest finally expelled from his living, and as an alchemist. Henry, a fine mystical poet, read Law and held the sedate post of secretary to Judge Lloyd. Thomas, interested in spiritual matters and a keeper of a vivid dream diary, experimented and worked at alchemy under the patronage of another famous 'chymist' of the day, Sir Robert Murrey, Secretary of State for Scotland. He wrote frequently under the pseudonym of 'Eugenius Philalethes'; his style is stirring, though he lacks the polish of his more poetical brother. He exhorts us to follow the path of Christianity as revealed through the alchemical teachings:

> Truth calls to man: 'Be ye transmuted ... be ye transmuted from dead stones into living philosophical stones. I am the true Medicine, rectifying and transmuting that which is no more into that which it was before corruption, and into something better by far, and that which is not into that which it ought to be. Lo, I am at the door of your conscience, knocking night and day, and ye will not open unto me, yet I stand mildly waiting ... Come again and again, often come, ye who seek wisdom ... O sonorous voice, O voice sweet and gracious to the ears of the sage, O fount of inexhaustible riches to those thirsting after truth and justice! O solace to the need of those who are desolate! Why seek ye further, anxious mortals?'[8]

Henry Vaughan, the poet, certainly understood the hermetic practice, but it is not known to what extent he carried out alchemical experiments. In his poetry he drew upon the mystical aspects of alchemy: poems such as

'The Night', 'Cock-crowing', or 'A Vision of Time and Eternity' provide convincing evidence that Vaughan was using alchemy not simply as a literary device, but that he had a deep understanding of its inner meaning and used this to fire his creative work.

ALCHEMY AND PHILOSOPHY

From the late fifteenth century onwards, a general movement arose in European circles of learning and nobility that attempted to draw together all the strands of artistic, scientific and occult disciplines, and to weave them into one universal system of knowledge.

One major stimulus to the formation of a universal philosophy was the rediscovery of the hermetic texts in 1460. Cosimo de' Medici of Italy (see p. 74) was at that time employing agents to scour the world for lost classics from the ancient Greek and Egyptian worlds. A monk presented him with a manuscript that proved to be a collection of many of the 'lost' texts ascribed to **Hermes Trismegistus**, a body of work now known as the *Corpus Hermeticum*. Hermes, closely associated with the Egyptian god Thoth, was said to have been a great Egyptian priest who had lived centuries before Christ. The writings under his name were widely revered, for here, it was thought, were the genuine and original teachings of Egypt, which apparently affirmed the truth of Christianity by referring to the existence of the divine Son.

Unfortunately, it was later discovered by Isaac Casaubon in 1614 that the texts did not pre-date Christ. We now know them to be the products of the first two or three centuries AD, composed by Greeks and containing strong Gnostic, Jewish and Neoplatonic influences. They may well contain elements of far earlier teachings, but they do not enshrine the wisdom of ancient Egypt. Nevertheless, even after 1614, they continued to exert a considerable fascination for alchemists and occult philosophers, the subtleties of observation and grandeur of cosmology being valued on their own account. They affirmed the principle of alchemy that Nature was the divine force of change operating within the Universe:

The Kosmos also . . . has sense and thought; but its sense and thought are of a kind peculiar to itself, not like the sense and thought of man, nor varying like his, but mightier and less diversified. The sense and thought of the Kosmos are occupied solely in making all things, and dissolving them again into itself. The Kosmos is an instrument of God's will.[9]

Man, the hermetic texts say, was created a being like God himself, made of Life and Light. He came to know the 'administrators', the planets that rule over destiny, and 'received a share of their nature'. But through will, he penetrated further into the created levels of the world, further into the realms of matter, until he was revealed to Nature. Nature fell in love with man, and enticed him to live on her earth.

The task of Man is to have the courage and will to develop his powers and attain to knowledge:

If then you do not make yourself equal to God, you cannot apprehend God; for like is known by like. Leap clear of all that is corporeal, and make yourself grow to a like expanse with that greatness which is beyond all measure; rise above all time and become eternal; then you will apprehend God. Think that for you too nothing is impossible; deem that you too are immortal, and that you are able to grasp all things in your thought, to know every craft and science; find your home in the haunts of every living creature; make yourself higher than all heights and lower than all depths, bring together in yourself all opposites of quality, heat and cold, dryness and fluidity; think that you are everywhere at once, on land, at sea, in heaven; think that you are not yet begotten, that you are in the womb, that you are young, that you are old, that you have died, that you are in the world beyond the grave; grasp in your thought all this at once, all times and places, all substances and qualities and magnitudes together; then you can apprehend God. But if you shut up your soul in your body, and abase yourself, and say 'I know nothing, I can do nothing; I am afraid of earth and sea, I cannot mount to heaven; I know not what I was, nor what I shall be', then what have you to do with God?[10]

On this basis, there was nothing to be ashamed of in alchemy, for what was it but a search for God through his manifestations in Nature, carried out with the power of thought and skill of craft that God had bestowed on man so that he might understand better the secrets of the creation? In another respect, it did away with the old emphasis on choosing alchemy itself as a pathway, as a mistress the alchemist served with unceasing devotion. Men of learning chose more and more to combine occult arts and rational sciences in their quest for an ever wider world view. They were not content to be bound by the obscure world of the laboratory and the daily attention to lengthy alchemical operations.

The opening up of alchemy, and its incorporation into new philosophies and schools of learning, meant that it provided a powerful leavening for the seekers of the period but became less and less distinguishable as a practice in its own right. For instance, it was a vital ingredient of Rosicrucianism, an esoteric movement that first came to prominence in 1614–15, when two texts – the *Fama Fraternitatis* and the *Confessio Fraternitatis* – appeared that told a strange tale of a secret society and a brotherhood that was ready to meet the dawning of a new age: 'Now there remains yet that which in short time . . . shall be spoke and uttered forth, when the World shall awake out of her heavy and drowsy sleep, and with an open heart, bare-head, and bare-foot, shall merrily and joyfully meet the new arising Sun.' The tale told in the *Fama* is that of one Brother Rosenkreuz (RC) who, a century or two before, had travelled widely in search of wisdom and learning and had founded an Order whose members were to devote themselves to this end.

The anonymous writer declared that the Order was still in existence, fortified by the recent discovery of the tomb of RC, which is described in precise and complex detail, indicating that it was laid out more as an occult temple than a grave. He implied that the Brethren were now seeking those of like mind to join them in preparation for the advent of wisdom into the world. The wisdom as formulated by the Order was to be of universal relevance, a synthesis of the best and most profound philosophy known to man. It would be 'a compendium of the Universe', the 'perfection [of] all Arts', 'so that finally man might thereby understand his own nobleness and worth, and why he is called Microcosmus, and how far his knowledge extendeth into Nature'.

The response was overwhelming. Many people wrote and published letters begging to be taken into the Order, while others condemned the heresy and presumption of the Brethren. No one openly admitted to being a member of the Order, but yet there soon grew up a body of literature and art that we can now classify as 'Rosicrucian'. It developed its own themes and identity, tying together cabbalism, Christianity, alchemy and astrology, as well as music, mathematics, geometry and architecture. As time went on, the reality of Rosicrucian brotherhoods was more readily admitted (one of the most intriguing by name being an American branch entitled The Woman in the Wilderness, devoted chiefly to the practice of spiritual alchemy), but by the mid-eighteenth century the early freshness and vitality had gone out of the concepts and emblems.

The works of writers such as Michael Maier, Heinrich Khunrath and Robert Fludd typify Rosicrucian literature and show how large a part alchemy played in it. According to one authority, **Heinrich Khunrath**, although he died in 1605, before the official 'launch' of Rosicrucianism, 'bears within the compass of his books all the elements that we recognise later in the Rosicrucian publications'.[11] He was in contact with, among others, John Dee and Emperor Rudolf of Prague, both of whom are thought to form links in the Rosicrucian chain. His *Amphitheatre of Eternal Wisdom*, with its very fine engravings, is a good example of how Rosicrucian illustrations differed from those of traditional alchemy. The latter usually set out to illustrate each stage of the alchemical process in turn. The Rosicrucians tend to give a complete picture of the quest in each illustration, including as many aspects as possible. For instance, in the engravings 'The Journey to the Heights' and 'The Castle of the Mysteries', the whole search is shown from start to finish, with aspirants setting out, working, travelling by boat, meeting with others, contemplating, praying, and so on. The landscapes are complex, and symmetry, proportion and perspective are used to make symbolic points. Khunrath did not neglect alchemy proper. A laboratory is shown in detail in 'The First Stage of the Great Work', but the room is also equipped with an oratory (in which the aspirant is shown praying) as well as musical and mathematical equipment. Alchemy was thus no longer seen as an exclusive art; it was brought into line with other disciplines in order to create a harmonious philosophy.

The Rosicrucian manifestos mention alchemy by name, and they curse the blindness of those who seek gold as a goal in its own right. It is the province of 'many runagates and roguish people [who] use great villainies and cozen and abuse the credit which is given them'. Those who want merely to transmute metals are not true philosophers. But Brother RC himself understood the art:

> Whatsoever has been said in the *Fama* concerning the deceivers against the transmutation of metals, and the highest medicine in the world, the same is thus to be understood, that this is so great gift of God we do in no manner set at naught, or despise it. But because she bringeth not with her always the knowledge of Nature, but this bringeth forth not only medicine, but also maketh manifest and open unto us innumerable secrets and wonders. Therefore it is requisite, that we be earnest to attain to the understanding and knowledge of philosophy. And moreover, excellent wits ought not to be drawn to the tincture of metals, before they be exercised well in the knowledge of Nature.[12]

We have little evidence of how the Rosicrucians applied their philosophy and learning in terms of individual development. The only clues come from writers who seem to bear the Rosicrucian identity, even if they do not admit to being one of the brotherhood. Such a one is **Robert Fludd** (1574–1637). He was the son of Sir Thomas Fludd, a military administrator, and was educated at Oxford. In 1598 he spent six years travelling as a tutor on the Continent, during which time he probably developed his medical and occult interests, partly through contact with Paracelsians (see Chapter 7). He returned to England

and took his degree in medicine, setting up practice in London, and was renowned for his successful personal effect upon his patients. But he came into conflict with the medical authorities because of his unorthodox views and his bluntness in expressing them. Fludd was celibate and devoted himself entirely to his medical practice and to his exploration of philosophy through his knowledge of music, alchemy and science. His greatest work is the *History of the Macrocosm and the Microcosm*, in which he attempts to describe the divine and the human worlds and the way in which they interact.

Fludd did not openly admit to membership of the Rosicrucian Order, but he wrote an essay in their defence that expounded their virtues and the necessity of

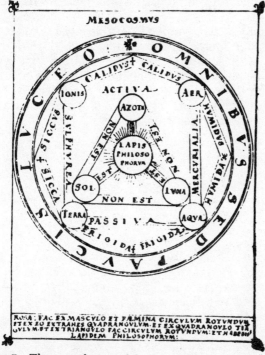

Fig. 7   The completion of the Great Work is shown in geometric form; all the elements are brought into harmony and the Philosopher's Stone created. (From Sylva Philosophorum, a seventeenth-century work by Cornelius Petraeus.)

accomplishing the 'mystical building' of the rose and the cross for oneself:

> The Alchemist transmutes the apparent forms into occult ones by finding the general form through destruction of the specific one. This is the work of the true and divine Alchemy, through the mediation of which the earthly has been opened to the entry of the joys of Paradise so that men may pluck that red rose with the lilies of the field and taste of the Tree of Life.

A spiritual, and Christian, form of alchemy, seems to have been a central theme for Fludd, and it may be that he distinguished this from 'laboratory' alchemy, which, in his diagrams, he lists equally with other arts and sciences, describing it only as 'art correcting Nature in the mineral realm'.

Alchemy thus expanded from a closely-knit discipline, into a tool for scientific and biological understanding, as well as into a spiritual teaching that was no longer dependent upon work carried out in a laboratory, and from the seventeenth century the history of 'pure' alchemy becomes harder to follow as it merges with other philosophies and traditions.

7 · APPLIED ALCHEMY

Alchemy has borne fruit in the realms of medicine, science and literature. Many of those who have been inspired by its philosophy and imagery were themselves practising alchemists, but often their alchemical skills have been overshadowed by their successes in the more conventional areas of the sciences and arts. There is a tendency to reject the tree which bore the fruit; the view is frequently taken by contemporary writers that the sole function of alchemy was to provide a starting point for the more 'objective' sciences. The more esoteric aspects of alchemy are often regarded as the necessary, but rather regrettable, means by which alchemy grew until it could be turned into a proper science. However since alchemy has been a source of inspiration for physicists, doctors, mystics, writers and psychologists, its power as a way of knowledge in its own right must surely be recognised. Alchemy rests on principles that have a deep relevance to man's work and progress in the world. The principles may be clothed in forms which are archaic or even erroneous in their assumptions, but these do not invalidate the principles themselves. Alchemy is like a central spindle, from which threads are unwound and taken into other contexts; they may eventually sever their original connection; but the spindle remains, and can be used again after years of neglect.

PARACELSUS AND ALCHEMICAL MEDICINE

Theophrastus Bombastus von Hohenheim, better known as Paracelsus (1493–1541), was born near Zurich and grew up in Villach (now in Austria). The whole course of his life was marked by an avid curiosity to learn at first hand, and to investigate and experiment without being tied to traditional doctrines. His first known phase of study began when he joined Sigismund Fugger, proprietor of mines and metal workshops in the Tyrol; here he learnt techniques of mining and the ways of using minerals and metals. Fugger himself was an alchemist, so alchemy was probably a very early topic of study for Paracelsus.

Training in occult matters may have come about as a result of contact with **Johannes Trithemius** (1462–1516), abbot of the monastery at Sponheim, an unusually learned and open-minded man who had been instructed in the secret sciences in his youth. He built up a magnificent library at the Abbey; his own learning embraced the Cabbala and Neoplatonic doctrines. As might be expected, he was at times accused of practising black magic, but he defended his position with the words: 'I am a lover of Divine Wisdom – in man and in Nature. This is the Magic I follow.' His pupils are thought to have included Cornelius Agrippa, the famous occultist and his writings such as the *Steganographia*, a treatise on angelic beings and astrology, were eagerly sought after by men such as John Dee.

We can infer from influences such as those of Fugger and Trithemius that Paracelsus was determined to expand his sphere of knowledge and bring the very highest and best into the medicine he practised. He also had a great respect for the native wisdom of peasants and gypsies, whom he saw as true observers of Nature. He had no respect for authority or academia, was badly dressed, frequently drunk, and always ready to quarrel. He travelled widely throughout Europe, possibly in the East as well, and his claim to have taken the last boat out from Rhodes before the Turkish invadion might link him with the Knights of St. John (see p.55). His professional status reached its peak when he was offered the post of City Physician and Professor of Medicine at Basel University after he had cured Johann Froben, a well-to-do printer who had been suffering from a serious and perplexing illness.

But Paracelsus soon made himself unpopular by refusing to worship at the shrine of Galen, Avicenna and Aristotle, whose writings were accorded the authority of Scripture by the medical practitioners of the day. He even burnt some of the sacred volumes in public and insulted the unquestioning physicians of his time in almost everything he wrote, calling them 'sausage-stuffers', 'clownish concocters', 'imposters' and 'ignorant sprouts'! After an unhappy law suit, Paracelsus left Basel in a hurry and spent most of his remaining years travelling in Germany and Austria. After his death in 1541 his followers grew in number until by about 1570 a definite Paracelsian school existed, and his influence has since spread; he is now considered as a key figure in the birth not only of modern orthodox medicine but also of homeopathic medicine.

His writings are numerous and complex, and it is not clear which are original works and which were composed by his pupils. Today there is a tendency to label his interests separately as alchemy, astrology, pharmacy or magic, but Paracelsus considered that they all should interact if medicine was to be effective.

A key feature of Paracelsian alchemical medicine was the importance of celestial energies and influences. Planets and metals were closely associated; gold, for instance, was said to be influenced by the sun as it grew to perfection in the earth and was itself an emblem of solar power. Each metal was related to a specific planet and was said to contain within itself an 'arcanum', a celestial power derived directly from its ruling planet. This arcanum could be released and perfected through the alchemical process and then used as an effective medicine. Modern chemists view this as the first real attempt to select out the active ingredient in a substance through chemical processes.

Carrying out such alchemical work, Paracelsus maintained, was like recreating the Universe in miniature. The right conditions in the vessel must be engendered so that the precise arcanum will manifest itself, just as the corresponding planet came to birth in the original creation of the world. He said that the alchemical furnace should be made like the firmament itself, 'fit and apt for the motion of Matter'. Within this, the glass vessel is placed like an inner firmament, and inside this the desired creation may take place. The work of alchemy is not primarily to make gold and silver:

> Its special work is this – To make arcana, and direct these to disease . . . The physician . . . must judge the nature of Medicine according to the stars . . . Since Medicine is worthless save in so far as it is from heaven, it is necessary that it shall be derived from heaven . . . Know, therefore, that it is arcana alone which are strength and virtues. They are, moreover, volatile substances, without bodies; they are a chaos, clear, pellucid, and in the power of a star.[1]

Ordinary herbal brews, said Paracelsus, were unlikely to be of great value since medicine should be of a subtle and potent composition, the original substance having undergone genuine transformation. Man himself has a level of being that corresponds to the celestial; therefore, if he is ill harmony should be restored at this level rather than at the gross physical level only:

> The third fundamental part, or pillar of true medicine, is Alchemy. Unless the physician be perfectly acquainted with, and experienced in this art, everything that he devotes to the rest of his art will be vain and useless. Nature is so keen and subtle in her operations that she cannot be dealt with except by a sublime and accurate mode of treatment. She brings nothing to the light that is at once perfect in itself, but leaves it to be perfected by man. This method of perfection is called Alchemy. For the Alchemist is a baker, in that he bakes bread; a wine merchant, seeing that he prepares wine; a weaver, because he produces cloths. So, whatever is poured forth from the bosom of Nature, he who adapts it to that purpose for which it is destined is an Alchemist.[2]

Paracelsus taught that the body itself is an alchemist. It transforms food and uses the beneficial substances, eliminating the rest. Here again Paracelsus was ahead of his time from the scientific point of view in seeing a relationship between chemistry and biochemistry. And from alchemy, he took the principle that a poison may contain much that is good within it. Poison, he said, is a relative term: 'Remember that God has formed all things perfect, in so far as regards their utility to themselves, but imperfect to others. Herein rests the foundation of the entity of poison.'

Arguing that what could be a poison in its gross form could also be a powerful medicine when prepared correctly, he went against the traditional Galenic view of curing through opposites. He maintained that the arcanum of a substance could be used to cure the evil effects which the substance itself produced. This is echoed in modern homeopathy, where minute doses of a substance are given to cure symptoms that correspond to those that the same substance would provoke if taken in a larger quantity: Belladonna, for instance, in a homeopathic dilution, may be used to treat delirium and fever – standard symptoms of belladonna poisoning – even though the patient has not in fact taken belladonna in its normal form. Homeopathy also follows the attempt of Paracelsus to work in the subtler realms of matter and mind, since the doses are so diluted that they pass beyond the level of normal measurable chemical dosage and may be said to correspond, broadly speaking, to the Paracelsian 'quintessence' or arcanum of the matter and to affect, accordingly, a deeper level of the patient's metabolism, a level at which psyche and body interact.

SCIENCE AND ALCHEMY

Alchemy always maintained a connection with the more practical arts of pharmacy and metallurgy. Frequently, processes initiated in the alchemical laboratory have emerged eventually into the everyday world as significant discoveries. A fine example, drawn to our attention by Sherwood Taylor, is that of the distillation of alcoholic spirits. From about AD 100 until the thirteenth century, distillation was exclusively an alchemical process; pharmacists of the time only used extraction, rather than the chemical technique of vaporizing and condensing. In the early Middle Ages alchemy went a step further and distilled wine into *aqua ardens* – brandy, a commonplace to us, but a marvel when it was first discovered. It was a manifestation of the alchemical aspiration to combine the two elements of fire and water, for it was both liquid and inflammable. Its medicinal powers were also found to be great, stimulating warmth and recovery from shock. Alcoholic spirits could also be used to preserve other organic materials and to extract essential oils from plants.

A list of achievements contributed by alchemy to science is given in *The Morning of the Magicians* by Pauwels and Bergier. They include: the production of potassium lye by Albert le Grand (1193–1280), the discovery of sodium sulphate by Johann Glauber (1604–68), of benzoic acid by Blaise Vigenere (1523–96), the recognition of gases by Johann-Baptiste Van Helmont (1577–1644), and the production of tin monoxide by G. della Porta (1541–1615).

The most potent and fascinating fusion of alchemy and science, however, came in the seventeenth and early eighteenth centuries with the work of eminent scientists such as Robert Boyle and Sir Isaac Newton. Both practised alchemy, both were inspired by its creed and both claimed to have achieved alchemical results. For these, and other scientists of the period, alchemy and science were bound up together, with alchemy influencing, and being influenced by, mechanical theories of matter, and science itself resting on a basis of mysticism and metaphysics. To the seventeenth-century mind, the worlds of nature, man and the divinity were inseparably related, and to study one without acknowledging the others was considered to be a distortion of the truth. **Sir Isaac Newton** (1642–1727) was born into a Lincolnshire family. A scholarly uncle took an interest in his education, sending him first to school at Grantham and then to Cambridge, where he eventually became a Fellow of Trinity College. His public reputation was high: he was made

Warden of the Mint in 1696 and knighted in 1705, by which time he was also President of the Royal Society.

Newton is best known now for his formulation of the theory of gravity, his discovery of the spectrum in white light, and his laws of planetary motion. But he was also a mystic and an alchemist, versed in hermetic teachings, the Cabbala and Neoplatonism. He was probably in contact with Henry More and Isaac Barrow, who were themselves Neoplatonists and in touch with alchemical circles in London. Newton was a secretive and reserved man, and it is only through his numerous unpublished papers and through scattered contemporary references that we have access to his alchemical thought and practice. He had a well-stocked library of alchemical books, and maintained his own laboratory. When a biography of Newton was being prepared after his death, his former assistant, Dr Humphrey Newton, ventured this reminiscence:

> He very rarely went to bed till *two* or *three* of the clock, sometimes not until *five* or *six*, lying about *four* or *five* hours, especially at spring and fall of the leaf, at which times he used to employ about six weeks in his laboratory, the fire scarcely going out either night or day; he sitting up one night and I another, till he had finished his chemical experiments, in the performances of which he was the most accurate, strict, exact. What his aim might be I was not able to penetrate into, but his pains, his diligence at these set times made me think he aimed at something beyond the reach of human art and industry ... Nothing extraordinary, as I can remember, happened in making his experiments; which, if there did, he was of so sedate and even temper, that I could not in the least discover it.[3]

(The references here to work in the spring and autumn correspond to the traditional alchemical times for starting the Great Work at the equinoxes.) But Newton *did* claim to have achieved success in making the philosophical mercury:

I know whereof I write, for I have in the fire manifold glasses with gold and this mercury. They grow in these glasses in the form of a tree, and by a continued circulation the trees are dissolved again with the work into a new mercury. I have such a vessel in the fire with gold thus dissolved, where the gold was visibly not dissolved through a corrosive into atoms, but extrinsically and intrinsically into a mercury as living and mobile as any mercury found in the world. For it makes the gold begin to swell, to be swollen and to putrefy, and also to spring forth into sprouts and branches, changing colours daily, the appearances of which fascinate me everyday.[4]

In other words, Newton was acknowledging current atomic theory of matter but was also stating that matter can be broken down in another way and that transformations can take place that by-pass the atomic process of combination.

Several of Newton's contemporaries brought alchemy out into the open and endeavoured to formulate its laws in the context of the new spirit of scientific enquiry. **Samuel Hartlib**, resident in England since 1625, was the focus of a circle of keen experimenters who compared results and discussed metaphysical and scientific theories, trying to find a synthesis and a balance between them. A laboratory was set up in Hartlib's back kitchen, and, in more gracious fashion, the enthusiasts also met at Ragley, the stately home of Lord and Lady Conway, who were keenly interested in such matters.

Robert Boyle (1627–91), who moved away from the old, secretive, esoteric way of working, caused great concern to Newton by his frank and open attitude. Boyle thought that he too had succeeded in making philosophic mercury, but Newton prayed that he would keep silence, for such a secret was 'not to be communicated without immense damage to ye world if there should be any verity in ye Hermetick writers'. Boyle's attitude was very different: '[If] the Elixir be a secret, that we owe wholly to our Maker's revelation, not our own industry, me thinks we should not so much grudge to impart what we did not labour to acquire, since our Saviour's prescription in the like case was this: Freely ye have received, freely give.'[5]

Boyle was later to write *The Sceptical Chymist*, in which he attacked the classical view that matter consisted of the four elements and substituted the definition of an element as that which cannot be broken down into any further substances. Whether he considered that alchemy was still a workable principle on this basis is uncertain. In Newton's case, however, research has shown that his knowledge of alchemy and hermeticism was a direct trigger for his discoveries in the realm of physics (see Betty Dobbs: *The Foundation of Newton's Alchemy*, CUP 1975). Without the study of alchemy and mysticism, Newton could not have made the discoveries that he did; nor did he consider that such discoveries invalidated the occult basis of science.

Chemistry took over from alchemy the accumulated knowledge of laboratory equipment, of chemical processes such as distillation, sublimation and coagulation, and all the formulas, materials and techniques that dealt exclusively with the physical properties of matter and identifiable chemical changes. Alchemy had been based upon personal effort, religious devotion and revelation, whereas the new chemistry took as its criteria experiments that could be repeated and theories that could be considered as proven only when identical results happened under identical conditions. Chemistry took the principle of careful observation from alchemy, but denied that the observer could affect the experiment or be involved in it himself. From the mid-eighteenth century onwards, anyone who tried to mix alchemy and chemistry was courting disaster. The unfortunate James Price, commanded to prove the transmuting powers of a powder which he claimed changed mercury into gold, committed suicide by swallowing prussic acid rather than face the sceptical eyes of the Fellows of the Royal Society.

There is no doubt that alchemy could not be called an objective science, as science was defined in the eighteenth and nineteenth centuries. But with contemporary science now undergoing a radical shift of viewpoint, and with our fundamental notions of the realities of time, space and matter all being revised and gaining – once more – a metaphysical aspect, alchemical concepts may yet provide future science with insights into the nature of the universe.

ALCHEMY AND LITERATURE

The drama of the alchemical process made fine material for literary adaptation. It has been said that the essence of drama is conflict, and in alchemy conflict leads to transformation through a sequence of different states. The themes of elemental conflict, death of the body, the triumphal union of the king and queen, and the growth of a precious elixir could serve as a structure for expressions of love, tragedy and Christian revelation. On a lighter note, the delusions of the naive alchemist and the trickery of the fraudulent transmuter provided material for satirical comedy, the most famous example of which is *The Alchemist* by **Ben Jonson** (1572–1637). However much Jonson may have ridiculed alchemy, he knew his subject well and could play with its images and implications in an intricate and subtle fashion, as Charles Nicholl has shown in *The Chemical Theatre*. Moreover, in *Eastward Hoe* Jonson and his co-authors used alchemical principles to provide a psychological structure for the drama; the characters of Frank Quicksilver, Master Golding and William Touchstone are defined by the alchemical associations with their names. Nicholl says:

> The naming of Quicksilver and Golding is not only a means of defining what they are ... but of suggesting what will happen to them. It also provides a formula for interaction, for as well as having individual chemical properties, mercury and gold had a specific relationship. By introducing a symbolic framework of chemical process and reaction, the authors of *Eastward Hoe* [Jonson, Marston and Chapman] turn the essentially static humour-portrayal into an active participant in the play's unfolding.[6]

There are strong indications that **Shakespeare** also used alchemy to give form and texture to his dramatic themes in certain plays. There is no doubt that he was acquainted with occult traditions;[7] he was well-versed in the Christian Cabbala, astrology, magic, and it seems, alchemy. It must remain speculation as to what extent Shakespeare practised any of these subjects, but it is clear that he had enough insight into them to weave them skilfully into his writing.

A Midsummer Night's Dream, for instance, can be interpreted successfully as an alchemical drama, as the Theatre Set-Up company proved in their research and 1983 production. Their conclusion was that Shakespeare used a heady mixture of Celtic lore and alchemy to give the 'Dream' its enchanting quality. Programme notes point to the theme of the four lovers, who to reach true harmony and a proper relationship must first be set in conflict with one another, just as the first material must be broken down if it is to be transformed:

> The 'subject matter' or 'raw stuff' (often symbolized by a serpent, dragon or toad and called 'earth' or 'lead') was thought to consist of the elements fire, air, water and earth. These appear in the names of the four lovers; fire in 'Helen' (torch of reeds), air in 'Hermia' (female of Hermes – the Greek for Mercury, whose element was air), water in 'Lysander' (from the chemical loosening as in *catalyst* – hence the liquid vitriol and water), and earth in 'Demetrius' (son of Demeter, earth-goddess), who thus becomes a subject matter of alchemical process. Helen as fire (often symbolized as a dog – hence 'I am your spaniel') is also his soul (symbolized as a dove, which she is called) or *anima* from which he must be separated, while his 'grossness' is purged and his change tested until he can be re-animated, as an improved person, and awaken to a 'golden dawn of concluding harmony'.

There are three sets of weddings in the play: that of Theseus and Hippolyta, the royal pair, that of the two couples just discussed, and then the union of Titania and Oberon, who had become estranged. This too is resonant with alchemical allegory, and the three levels can be seen as body, soul and spirit, all of which must complete the perfect change if the alchemical process is to succeed. The union of Titania and Oberon may be interpreted as representing the body, since they are themselves nature spirits, that of the four lovers as signifying the soul (which in alchemy needs the most careful and complex handling), and that of the royal pair as the spirit. The spirit, or 'sulphur', requires less transformation than the other two, needing rather to be brought out from obscurity and affirmed just as Hippolyta, Queen of the Amazons, has been led out from her fierce and distant country by Theseus. Puck is the means by which all the trouble is stirred up, the cause of mischief and misunderstanding: 'The agent of alchemy was Mercury, who "led" the subjects and practised upon them, beginning and finishing the work. This is Puck's function and psychologically he is he "psychopomp" leading the souls, like Virgil in Dante's *Inferno*.'[8] Mercury was depicted as totally volatile, changeable and elusive, taking the symbolic forms of different beasts, birds and figures in alchemical illustration. This corresponds precisely to Puck's gleeful speech when he upsets the rustics at their play rehearsal and scatters them into flight in the forest.

> I'll follow you, I'll lead you about a round,
> Through bog, through bush, through brake, through brier:
> Sometimes a horse I'll be, sometime a hound,
> A hog, a headless bear, sometimes a fire;
> And neigh, and bark, and grunt, and roar, and burn,
> Like horse, hound, hog, bear, fire, at every turn.

So through the powers of Mercury, unleashed by the alchemist (in this case perhaps corresponding to Oberon, who is Puck's master), the four elements are set at war with one another, and then reunited in perfect balance. Titania is humbled and overcomes her pride to become Oberon's consort once more; the three levels of marriage take place and the work is perfected.

In *King Lear*, also by Shakespeare, Charles Nicholl similarly detects another alchemical theme, with Lear himself as the subject of transformation through his renunciation of power, paternal love and even his sight. His mortification is complete, his own death is the ultimate tragedy, yet through his trials and death evil has been purged from the kingdom. The concluding 'golden' harmony is not as obvious in *King Lear* as in *A Midsummer Night's Dream*, but alchemical purgation of the gross and exalting of the fine has indeed taken place. Nicholl points out that Lear's daughter, Cordelia, is like the alchemical material that is despised and mistaken for poison, and yet is the most precious balm of all. Dismissed from the scene early on, she is like the portion of Mercurial water that must be reserved in the alchemical work until it is needed for restoration and nurturing of the injured, mortified matter. Her tears, flowing for her father, are like the alchemical dew that is impregnated with powerful natural force:

> All bless'd secrets,
> All you unpublish'd virtues of the earth,
> Spring with my tears!

Later, her kisses are seen as a healing balm:

> O my dear father! Restoration, hang
> Thy medicine on my lips, and let this kiss
> Repair those violent harms that my two sisters
> Have in thy reverence made![10]

A more overt use of alchemical imagery can be found in the poetry of the sixteenth and seventeenth centuries: **John Donne** (1573–1631) frequently utilised alchemical themes in his work. In 'A Nocturnall upon S. Lucie's Day' he compares his state to that of the material that has absorbed light and moisture and now lies blackening in the vessel, dying to be reborn as the elixir:

> Study me then, you who shall lovers bee
> At the next world, that is, at the next Spring:
> For I am every dead thing,
> In whom love wrought new Alchimie.
> For his art did expresse
> A quintessence even from nothingnesse,
> From dull privations, and leane emptinesse
> He ruin'd mee, and I am re-begot
> Of absence, darknesse, death; things which are not.

George Herbert (1593–1633) and **Andrew Marvell** (1621–78) also used hermetic allusions in their verse, Herbert often in a simple and devout form, Marvell in a more speculative and philosophical vein. Herbert, for instance, begins his poem 'Easter' with the following lines:

Rise, heart; thy Lord is risen. Sing his praise
　　Without delays,
Who takes thee by the hand, that thou likewise
　　With him may'st rise;
That, as his death calcined thee to dust,
His life may make thee gold, and much more, Just.

One of the finest examples of a religious poem using alchemical symbolism is by **Robert Southwell** (1561?–95),
who in 'The Burning Babe' saw the alchemical furnace as
giving birth to Christ:

As I in hoarie Winters night stoode shivering in the
　　snow,
Surpris'd I was with sodaine heate, which made my hart
　　to glow;
And lifting up a fearefull eye, to view what fire was
　　neare,
A pretty Babe all burning bright did in the ayre
　　appeare;
Who scorched with excessive heate, such floods of
　　teares did shed,
As though his floods should quench his flames, which
　　with his teares were bred:
Alas (quoth he) but newly borne, in fierie heates I frie,
Yet none approach to warme their harts or feele my fire,
　　but I;
My faultless breast the furnace is, the fuell wounding
　　thornes:
Love is the fire, and sighs the smoake, the ashes, shames
　　and scornes;
The fewell Justice layeth on, and Mercie blowes the
　　coales,
The metall in this furnace wrought, are mens defiled
　　soules:
For which, as now on fire I am to worke them to their
　　good,
So will I melt into a bath, to wash them in my blood.
With this he vanisht out of sight, and swiftly shrunk
　　away,
And straight I called unto minde, that it was Christmass
　　day.

8 · THE PHOENIX:
ALCHEMY IN THE TWENTIETH CENTURY

The history of alchemy in the twentieth century is a fragmented one. Firstly, there has been a continuation of the practice of traditional alchemy; secondly an absorption of alchemy into esoteric teachings; thirdly, a reappraisal of alchemy in terms of psychology; and fourthly, an effort to relate alchemy to the frontiers of science. Let us look at each of these stories in turn.

TRADITIONAL ALCHEMY

Although traditional alchemy fell into a decline during the eighteenth and nineteenth centuries, it did not die out altogether. In the Islamic culture, especially, it was still practised in the time-honoured fashion. E. J. Holmyard, an expert on Islamic alchemy, relates that he was acquainted with certain twentieth-century practitioners, one of whom was a learned theologian named Abdul-Muhyi (he came to England and carried out his experiments, unsuccessfully it seems, in a blacksmith's forge in Surrey). Muhyi had contacts with alchemical circles: 'One of his last acts', wrote Holmyard, 'was to write a letter of introduction to an alchemist friend at Fez, the outcome of which was to give the author the privilege of being taken to see a subterranean alchemical laboratory in the old part of the city.' More than this, one surmises, he was not allowed to divulge.

Since the general opinion in Europe from the eighteenth century onwards was that alchemy was the occupation of lunatics and impostors, those who have carried out alchemical studies in the twentieth century have tended to keep quiet about their activities. Two of the best accounts of modern alchemy are by Armand Barbault and Archibald Cockren, both of whom seem to have come to alchemy from inner promptings, using historical texts for guidance, rather than by learning the discipline directly from a teacher.

Cockren's *Alchemy Rediscovered and Restored* (1940) contains a brief and over-generalised history of alchemy, but of far greater interest is a section in which he recounts his own alchemical experiments and eventual success. He worked with different metals over many years until he found the right one (unnamed) with which to begin the process of making the philosophical mercury:

> This metal, after being reduced to its salts and undergoing special preparation and distillation, delivered up the Mercury of the Philosophers, the Aqua Benedicta, the Aqua Celestis, the Water of Paradise. The first intimation I had of this triumph was a violent hissing, jets of vapour pouring from the retort and into the receiver like sharp bursts from a machine-gun, and then a violent explosion, whilst a very potent and subtle odour filled the laboratory and its surroundings. A friend has described this odour as resembling the dewy earth on a June morning, with the hint of growing flowers in the air, the breath of the wind over heather and hill, and the sweet smell of the rain on the parched earth.

Cockren then had to find a way of storing this subtle and volatile gas; he managed to condense it into a 'clear golden-coloured water'. Later, he added this to salts of gold and through distillation of the mixture obtained oil of gold, or potable gold. To obtain the white and the red elixir, further stages were necessary, which involved treating the black metallic residue left after the extraction of the golden water and calcining it. Cockren calls this the 'salt', to which he added the 'mercury' and the 'sulphur', these being the white and the red water he had obtained from the golden mercurial water. He mixed the three principles in appropriate quantities, sealed them into a flask, and subjected them to a regulated heat. I quote here from his description of the change in the vessel, since it corresponds very closely with Newton's account (see p. 106): 'On conjunction the mixture takes on the appearance of a leaden mud, which rises slowly like dough until it throws up a crystalline formation rather like a coral plant in growth. The "flowers" of this plant are composed of petals of crystal which are continually changing in colour.' From this point the process goes through the familiar stages of *nigredo*, conjunction, birth of the 'son', peacock's tail and finally the white then the red elixir.

Cockren was known to his contemporaries as a sincere and intelligent man; in addition he had a first-class professional scientific training, being a specialist in the field of physiotherapy and massage. His chief interest in alchemy was in its medical applications, and he follows Paracelsus in believing that all true medicine must be derived from purified substances, materials that have 'passed by fire to a second birth'.

Armand Barbault, a Frenchman, also regarded the greatest good of alchemy as the production of effective medicine. He seems to have been of a very different character from Cockren, however – something of a cult figure, a showman magician-alchemist as opposed to the retiring and shy Mr Cockren. His approach to alchemy is more original, and although he claimed to follow the signs and indications given in old texts and illustrations, yet he interpreted them very much in his own way. His account in *Gold of a Thousand Mornings* makes worthwhile reading, and brings out some interesting alchemical implications, especially concerning the role of astrology and the power of plants; but taken as a whole it is less convincing and definitely hovering more 'on the edge of the etheric' than Cockren's work.

Barbault worked almost exclusively with organic matter. His Primal Material, which he called the 'Philosopher's Peat', had to be gathered under correct locational and astrological conditions from about ten centimetres underneath the surface:

> What *is* this First Matter hidden several centimetres under the turf? Is it not – at least as far as the layman is concerned – plain ordinary earth? For the initiated person it is something quite different: it is *living* earth, seized from the ground by a very special process belonging to the sphere of High Magic, which allows the adept assigned to the task to gain possession of an entire collection of physical and metaphysical principles.

Barbault took much time and trouble gathering plants and dew for alchemical processing and for adding to the First Matter. Again, he was always careful that the time of day, the season and the planetary configurations were favourable so that the sap and the dew would be at maximum potency. Barbault had at one time been a fashionable professional astrologer, and he assessed each critical moment in the Great Work in detail, choosing a suitable horoscope for starting each stage of the process. Following the alchemical tradition he also believed that the practitioner's own chart was of vital importance. His horoscope, he boasted, proclaimed his special aptitude for a spiritualised science!

Barbault eventually perfected his elixir, and invited various professionals to test it, including the Weleda laboratories. The 'vegetable gold' apparently had extremely beneficial effects upon a number of patients suffering from different illnesses. He would have liked to have initiated full-scale production, but found that the cost of the operation needed was prohibitive. His conclusion was that his medicine was in a different category altogether from conventional medicine, although it had some connection with homoeopathic preparations: '[I realised] that my liquor of gold was not a specific remedy but a universal additive, able to stimulate the effects of ordinary medicine to a remarkable degree by acting on the entire vital field. My medicine does not, therefore, seek to operate on the same wave-length as official medicine.'

ALCHEMY AND ESOTERIC SCHOOLS

Alchemical teachings were absorbed into a number of twentieth-century esoteric teachings. Some occultists, like Barbault, saw in alchemy a potential magical framework, its ceremonial approach and vivid mythological imagery lending itself to the development of psychic abilities and the harnessing of subtle energies. Magic can be briefly defined as the process of learning to understand, manipulate and interpret energies that exist in ourselves and in the natural world. Most students of magical traditions would agree that magic itself is 'natural', but involves working at a higher level of awareness and sensitivity than normal; it involves great personal responsibility and unless it is practised with proper motivation and discrimination can become tainted with greed or delusion. In these broad terms, alchemy has a great affinity with magic in its emphasis upon releasing the active energy from material substances throught the dedication and correct outlook of the practitioner.

The Hermetic Order of the Golden Dawn incorporated alchemy into its occult teachings. The Order was founded in 1887, but it was still intensively active in the first two decades of the twentieth century and its influence may be perceived in many esoteric orders today. It is thought to have had Rosicrucian affiliations, but its origins are shrouded in myth and mystery like its purported antecedent. The Order was carefully structured, conducted on a basis of ordered learning programmes for its initiates, who moved up from one 'grade' to another as they mastered various systems and skills. The Cabbala was taught as was divination – mainly astrology and tarot. Symbols were painted, magical weapons made, robes sewn and complex rituals learnt by heart.

Those who wished to proceed through the Order's grades were expected to be familiar with alchemical symbolism and perhaps to have some experience of practical alchemy. With its emphasis on divination, symbolism and experience of 'higher planes', the

Golden Dawn concentrated more on the revelations that alchemy could bring rather than on its physical process. An instruction, probably written by S. L. MacGregor Mathers, a Chief of the Order, reads as follows:

> Before commencing any Alchemical process, and at the different stages of it, bring the Cucurbite, Retort, Crucible, or other vessel containing the Matter, place it in the centre of the table and range the Tablets round it thus: White Tablet with Head (North), Black and Grey Tablet with white pentacle (East), Tablet with Crystal (South), Coloured Tablet with Hexagram (West). (The Operator stands in the South.)
>
> Then endeavour according to the directions to see in the Crystal and go to the Alchemical plane corresponding under the Sephira of (Chokmah) where ask the Governor of Hylech to send down the Divine Light into the Matter, the LVX. Perform what other operations you wish and then remove the Tablets and continue the Alchemical processes as usual. In the intervals between the stages etc., act as here prescribed.
>
> Description of the Plane. A beautiful garden in which is a fountain issuing from a pillar and filling a large oblong basin with a certain white water. This place is guarded by an Angel with a Caducean Wand, who represents Metatron on this plane. Ask him to bring you before the Throne of the Governor of Hylech. Above the Pillar is a Globe and the Bird of Hermes human-headed. Further on is the throne of the Governor of Hylech who has rainbow colours about him. There are also near him the four Angels of the Elements, the Red King and White Queen etc. and many other symbolic forms. Ask the Governor of Hylech that the Divine LVX may be sent into the Matter and give as your symbols (the Pyramid) and (the Rose Cross).[1]

Probably the most important contribution that the Golden Dawn made to the alchemical tradition was in drawing out the potential of its symbolism, and in acknowledging its position as an integral part of the Western occult tradition. Without the Golden Dawn, it is quite possible that alchemy would have been quietly pensioned off. It may also be due to the work of the Golden Dawn, that many Western spiritual and occult disciplines today are imbued with some of the symbolism and terminology of alchemy. For instance, following the path of knowledge is often referred to as the 'Great Work', or simply 'the Work'. Modern descriptions of the Cabbalistic Tree of Life, too, draw on alchemical practice. The diagram of the Tree contains at its middle level a relationship between three points – Tiphareth (individuality), Geburah (judgement and strength) and Chesed (love and mercy), and it is often said that this triad is like a vessel in which the soul must be born after a man is purified by being stripped of false values and judgements and becoming receptive to the true quality of love.

G. I. Gurdjieff also presented the basic ideas of alchemy in his 'work', and used them in an original and inventive form. Gurdjieff was active first in Russia, then in France and America from the early years of the present century until his death in 1949. It is hard to summarise his teachings, which, like those of the Golden Dawn, have had a profound effect upon contemporary esoteric thinking and practice. Perhaps they could best be described as 'a science of consciousness', the teaching of a way through which man can 'wake up' to his possibilities through proper observation of himself and the world around and through effective direction of personal energies and emotions.

Gurdjieff taught that man possessed several 'centres' of consciousness, ranging from one of powerful instinct to ones of higher intellect and emotion. The body is not to be seen as a separate entity, but is connected to all these centres in specific and often subtle ways – the body is dense matter, whereas spirit is also matter, although very rarefied. He demonstrated that the body is a kind of factory that will convert the food that comes in to nourish itself. However, he did not restrict this to the notion of physical food, but taught that we take in three kinds of food – physical nourishment, air and impressions. We need all of these to stay alive. This Gurdjieff described as our own alchemy, the process by which we sift out the different elements and convert them into a form in which we can digest, store or use them in our physical, mental and emotional lives: 'This is our inner alchemy, the transmutation of base metals into precious metals.

But all this alchemy is inside us, not outside ... In man's inner alchemy higher substances are distilled out of other, coarser material which otherwise would remain in a coarse state.'[2]

PSYCHOLOGY AND ALCHEMY

In the field of psychology, alchemy has found a natural home. With the growing urge to explore human instincts and mental processes, it became apparent that the alchemical process could be seen as a description of inner transformation. While C. G. Jung (1875–1961), the Swiss psychologist, is the most famous interpreter of alchemy in this light, he was preceded by Major-General **E. A. Hitchcock** (1798–1870), an American, who scorned the idea that the transmutation of metals was the true aim of alchemy, holding instead that 'man was the subject of Alchemy; and that the *object* of the art was the perfection, or at least the improvement, of man!'[3]

Jung, however, is the most significant figure in the revival of alchemy in the twentieth century. Many people owe their interest in alchemical symbolism to his work, and his contribution to unlocking the language of alchemical emblems in terms of the human psyche cannot be over-valued. However, it would be short-sighted to assume that alchemical evolution comes to a halt with Jung; questions of the interaction of mind and matter were largely left untouched by him, and he had no interest in the actual laboratory operations of the alchemists.

Jung established the vital link between psychology and alchemy, and saw the imagery of alchemy as a description of the journey of the human soul. It was in dreams that he found the strongest connection, discovering a profound correspondence between alchemical emblems and imagery occurring spontaneously in dreams, especially those that mark times of crisis or transformation for the dreamer. In some of his patients' dreams he found an almost precise parallel with images used in old alchemical illustrations, even though the patients concerned had no knowledge of alchemy. His basic theory, which has deeply influenced many psychologists, artists, writers and thinkers ever since, is that the psyche of each person merges, at its deepest point, with the psyche of mankind as a whole (the 'collective unconscious') and that the human psyche – energy in its essence – crystallises into various fundamental images, which are beyond pictorial image in themselves ('archetypes') but which may surface in the form of a recognisable image or symbol in the consciousness of individual man, chiefly through the medium of dreams and visions. Jung saw that the alchemical symbols (such as the rose, the eagle, the king and queen, the fighting dragons) were themselves representatives of these archetypes and that the alchemists had, by means of these symbols, described the development of the human psyche itself from its 'raw' state into one of perfection, or gold.

Jung named this whole process 'individuation', and in doing so broke away from the prevalent theory that signs of disturbance in the individual were necessarily warnings of abnormality; he maintained that, like the alchemical process, the process of individual growth was one of conflict, crisis and change. He discovered that he could interpret certain of his patients' dreams as parallels of alchemical stages, and assess their current psychic state accordingly.

Jung was himself always willing to explore aspects of his own psyche, and to be affected by dreams and images. His discovery of alchemy emerged as part of his own personal development:

> Before I discovered alchemy, I had a series of dreams which repeatedly dealt with the same theme. Beside my house stood another, that is to say, another wing or annex, which was strange to me. Each time I would wonder in my dream why I did not know this house, although it had apparently always been there. Finally came a dream in which I reached the other wing. I discovered there a wonderful library, dating largely from the sixteenth and seventeenth centuries. Large, fat folio volumes, bound in pigskin, stood along the walls. Among them were a number of books embellished with copper engravings of a strange character, and illustrations containing curious symbols such as I had never seen before. At the time I did not know to what they referred; only much later did I

*Fig. 8   The Green Lion, symbol of the living force that
must be sought in the Prima Materia. (From Atlanta Fugiens
by Michael Maier.)*

recognize them as alchemical symbols. In the dream I was
conscious only of the fascination exerted by them and by
the entire library.[4]

Through his contact with alchemy Jung transformed his
own understanding of Christianity:

One night I awoke and saw, bathed in bright light at the foot
of my bed, the figure of Christ on the Cross. It was not quite
life-size, but extremely distinct and I saw that this body
was made of greenish gold. The vision was marvellously
beautiful, and yet I was profoundly shaken by it . . . [It]
came to me as if to point out that I had overlooked something in my reflections: the analogy of Christ with the
aurum non vulgi and the *viriditas* of the alchemists . . .
The green gold is the living quality which the alchemists
saw not only in man but also in organic nature. It is an

expression of the life-spirit, the *anima mundi* or *filius macrocosmi*, the *Anthropos* who animates the whole cosmos. This spirit has poured himself into everything, even into inorganic matter; he is present in metal and stone. My vision was thus a union of the Christ-image with his analogue in matter, the *filius macrocosmi*.[5]

In Jung we have an example of a man whose life and work was totally transformed by contact with the alchemical tradition. He could be called an alchemist of the psyche, the guiding Mercurius spirit who could lead men and women through the dangers and trials of the inner process of transformation.

SCIENCE AND ALCHEMY, OR 'PARACHEMISTRY'

The place of alchemy in modern science is hardly a prominent one; however, both the revival of interest in alchemy as a practical occult discipline, and the advances of the scientific world view mean that it is not entirely without a foothold there. Alchemy has its modern practitioners; although the cutting edge of scientific discovery, with all its sophisticated equipment, can hardly be exercised in one's back parlour, nevertheless there is a place for those who wish to try and integrate qualities of attention and inner vision with laboratory work. Likewise, in the field of complementary medicine, experiments are being conducted in the preparation of medicines with these principles in mind, processes in which prevailing planetary influences and state of mind of the operator are considered as having a potential influence on the efficacy of the remedy. (Readers are referred to issues of *The Hermetic Journal*, edited by Adam Maclean, for current progress in these areas.)

Whether alchemy can achieve physical results unknown to conventional science remains a moot point; certain twentieth-century adepts believe that it has as much power to wield as nuclear physics.

In *The Morning of the Magicians*, Jacques Bergier relates his account of a meeting in 1937 with a 'mysterious personage', an impressive and practising alchemist who warned him of the dangers of nuclear science, which was then in a critically expansive phase. He told Bergier that such experiments were fraught with dangers through explosive release of atomic energy and poisoning through radiation. His most startling pronouncement was that the alchemists themselves were in possession of this secret and had used the nuclear principle in their work for centuries – aeons, perhaps – but had done so from 'moral and religious' motivations, which had enabled them to handle the power in a responsible way. Bergier, who had been longing to meet a genuine alchemist, asked the stranger to instruct him as to the true nature of the art:

> You ask me to summarize for you in four minutes four thousand years of philosophy and the efforts of a life-time. Furthermore, you ask me to translate into ordinary language concepts for which such a language is not intended. All the same, I can tell you this much: you are aware that in the official science of today the role of the observer becomes more and more important. Relativity, the principle of indeterminacy, show the extent to which the observer today intervenes in all these phenomena. The secret of alchemy is this: there is a way of manipulating matter and energy so as to produce what modern scientists call 'a field of force'. This field acts on the observer and puts him in a privileged position *vis-à-vis* the Universe. From this position he has access to the realities which are ordinarily hidden from us by time and space, matter and energy. This is what we call 'The Great Work'.[7]

It may well be that alchemy knows another way of altering atomic structure without the use of huge and costly nuclear reactors, and possibly there are clues to this knowledge in the insistence on the almost endless repetition of certain parts of the process, such as distilling and re-distilling the liquid matter hundreds of times.

The philosophy of modern science could certainly now provide a more hospitable climate for alchemical concepts. The world view has grown; boundaries have been pushed back by the advent of new branches of science, including quantum physics, which breaks down the distinction between energy and matter, and demonstrates how the 'observer' is in reality a 'participator' in atomic experiment, affecting the very particles that are worked on.

> Quantum theory thus reveals a basic oneness of the universe. It shows that we cannot decompose the world into independently existing smallest units. As we penetrate into matter, nature does not show us any isolated 'basic building blocks' but rather appears as a complicated web of relations between the various parts of the whole. These relations always include the observer in an essential way. The human observer constitutes the final link in the chain of observational processes, and the properties of any atomic objects can only be understood in terms of the object's interaction with the observer. This means that the classical ideal of an objective description of nature is no longer valid . . . In atomic physics, we can never speak about nature without, at the same time, speaking about ourselves.[6]

Quantum physics is not alone in bringing in ideas of consciousness, and of unity. 'Chaos' theory opens out the possibility that one small action may have universal effects, and the concept of 'morphic resonance' (pioneered by Rupert Sheldrake) states that the individuals of a species are linked into a common field, which can both be influenced by the individual and can also transmit new knowledge to its members.

Further theories will doubtless arise. Not all will stand up to the test, but what does seem to be happening is that there is increasing motivation to develop a world picture which can include not only physical materiality, but time, space and consciousness as well. The old rigid boundaries between mind and matter have crumbled. These new scientific premises are close to those upon which alchemy is based; hence it seems possible that alchemy may still be able to yield new scientific insights, for those who take the trouble to look.

ALCHEMY – WHERE NEXT?

Alchemy is still feeding the general culture of the Western world. We have seen how it continues to illuminate and inspire arts, human behavioural studies, and science. It throws light on pre-existent forms, such as music and poetry, and serves as fuel for creating new ones. It could be argued, however, that these are spin-offs of alchemy, not the full practice of the tradition as it has been known. From this angle, we might say that alchemy is over; the elements of its practice, long-lived as they were, were subject to the conditions of time and society, conditions which have now dissolved.

However, we should also ask if perhaps the spirit of alchemy goes deeper even than the forms of alchemy as we know them. Traditions of knowledge weave their way quietly through aeons of cultural and religious change, and may change their outer forms so drastically that the continuity between one phase and the other is not recognised. The Cabbala, for instance, known officially as a Judaic and Judaeo-Christian mystery tradition, may well be deeper rooted than its official history proclaims; the Tree of Life, its chief symbol and cosmic glyph, is found in strikingly similar forms both in Assyrian mythology and in Egyptian symbolism.

The big question is then: what is alchemy? When all the outer forms are stripped away, what is left? If alchemy has to evolve a new form, it is from that underlying spirit that it will be fashioned. What can be discarded, without destroying the essence? Perhaps this essence cannot really be named; however, at its very simplest, the aim of alchemy is to transform base matter into gold. Now that we have reached the end of this particular survey of alchemy, it can readily be seen that this statement can be taken in many different ways. The future of alchemy may well depend on discovering yet another way in which it can be realised, perhaps something that, as yet, we can scarcely dream of.

REFERENCES

Abbreviations: HM = *The Hermetic Museum*, ed. A.E.Waite (1893)
TCB = *Theatrum Chemicum Britannicum*, Elias Ashmole (1652)

CHAPTER 1:

1. *The Sophic Hydrolith* (HM).
2. *The Golden Tripod* (HM).
3. Ibid.
4. Cockren, *Alchemy Discovered and Restored*, p. 138.

CHAPTER 2:

1. Sutherland, *Gold*.
2. Quoted in Lindsay, *The Origins of Alchemy*
3. H.J. Shepperd, 'Alchemy: Origin or Origins?', Ambix, vol. XVII (July 1970).
4. Ko Hung (c. AD 300) quoted in Needham, *Science and Civilisation in China.*

CHAPTER 3:

1. Thomas Norton, *The Ordinall of Alchimy* (1477); first published in English in 1652 (TCB).
2. Taylor, *Imagination and the Growth of Science.*
3. Cornelius Agrippa, *Of Occult Philosophy*, p. 511.
4. Quoted by Lindsay, *The Origins of Alchemy.*
5. *The Golden Tract* (HM).

CHAPTER 4:

1. Holmyard, *Alchemy*, p. 87.
2. From the *Corpus Hermeticum*, quoted by Lindsay, *The Origins of Alchemy.*

3. Norton, *The Ordinall of Alchimy* (1477, 1652).
4. From *Gloria Mundi* (1526), quoted by Read, *Prelude to Chemistry*.
5. *The Sophic Hydrolith* (HM).
6. Translated from Berthelot, *Collection des Anciens Alchimistes Grecs*.
7. HM.
8. *The Book of Lambspring* (HM).
9. *The Kabbalah Unveiled*, tr. S. L. MacGregor Mathers (Routledge & Kegan Paul 1970), p. 116.
10. See Adam McLean, 'The Birds in Alchemy', *The Hermetic Journal*, no. 5, p. 15.
11. John A. Mehung, *A Demonstration of Nature* (HM).
12. *The Golden Tripod* (HM).
13. Sir George Ripley, *The Compound of Alchemy* (TCB).
14. In TCB.
15. Barbault, *Gold of a Thousand Mornings*, p. 51–2.
16. Quoted in Sherwood Taylor, *The Alchemists*, p. 67.
17. Nicolas Flamel, *Explanation of the Hieroglyphicall Figures*.
18. Wei Po-yang (second century AD), quoted by C. G. Jung, *Alchemical Studies*.
19. *The Treatises of Philalethes* (HM).
20. Michael Sendivogius, *The New Chemical Light* (HM).
21. Pseudo-Geber, *The Sum of Perfection*.
22. Ripley, *The Compound of Alchemy*.

CHAPTER 5:

1. Denis Stevens, *The Letters of Claudio Monteverdi*.
2. Oliver Strunk, *Source Readings in Musical History*, Vol. 3, *The Baroque Era*.
3. Caccini, *Le nuove musiche 1602*, quoted in Strunk, op. cit.
4. British Library Manuscripts, *Splendor Solis*.
5. Stevens, op. cit.
6. Strunk, op. cit.
7. Foreword to *Madrigali Guerrieri ed Amorosi*, (Madrigals of War and Love), quoted in Strunk, op. cit.
8. Quoted in Strunk, op. cit.

CHAPTER 6:

1. Heinrich Nolle, *The Chemist's Key*, translation from the German attributed to Henry Vaughan (1657).
2. *The Secret of the Golden Flower*, tr. Wilhelm.
3. Frontispiece to *Musaeum Hermeticum* (1625).
4. Michael Sendivogius, *The New Chemical Light* (HM).
5. *Nicholas Flamel, his explanation of the hieroglyphicall figures*.
6. Quoted in *The Hermetic Journal*, no. 14 (Adam McLean, *Jacob Boehme*), p. 23, from the narrative of Manly Palmer Hall.
7. Boehme, *Signatura Rerum* (The Signature of All Things) (James Clarke & Co.), pp. 13, 89.
8. Thomas Vaughan, *The Magical Writings of Thomas Vaughan*, ed. A.E.

Waite (1974 Health Research), p. 64

9. *Corpus Hermeticum*, Libellus II, tr. Scott.
10. Ibid., Libellus XI.
11. Adam McLean, *The Hermetic Journal*, no. 12 (*Heinrich Khunrath*), p. 35.
12. *The Confession*, p. 132.

CHAPTER 7:

1. Paracelsus, *Alchemy, the Third Column of Medicine* (ed. A.E.Waite).
2. Ibid, p.148.
3. Quoted in Dobbs, *The Foundations of Newton's Alchemy*.
4. Ibid.
5. Ibid., p. 108.
6. Nicholl, *The Chemical Theatre*.
7. See Frances Yates, *The Occult Philosophy in the Elizabethan Age*.
8. Theatre Set-Up programme notes, 1983.
9. *King Lear*, IV,iv.
10. Ibid., IV, vii.

CHAPTER 8:

1. Gilbert, *The Golden Dawn*, pp. 65–6.
2. P. D. Ouspensky, *The Fourth Way* RKP p. 220.
3. Luther H. Martin Jnr., 'A History of the Psychological Interpretation of Alchemy', *Ambix* (March 1975).
4. Jung, *Memories, Dreams and Reflections*.
5. Ibid.
6. Capra, *The Tao of Physics*, p. 71.
7. Pauwels and Bergier, *The Morning of the Magicians*, p. 24.

SELECT BIBLIOGRAPHY

Key books for historical study:
Burland, C. A., *The Arts of the Alchemists* (Weidenfeld and Nicolson, 1967).
Holmyard, E. J., *Alchemy* (Pelican, 1957).
Lindsay, Jack, *The Origins of Alchemy in Graeco-Roman Egypt* (Frederick Muller, 1970).
Nicholl, Charles, *The Chemical Theatre* (RKP, 1980).
Read, John, *Prelude to Chemistry* (G. Bell and Sons Ltd, 1936).
Sherwood Taylor, F., *The Alchemists* (Paladin, 1976).

Alchemical texts – collections and single works
Allen, Paul M., *A Christian Rosenkreutz Anthology* (Rudolf Steiner Publications, 1968).
Ashmole, Elias, *Theatrum Chemicum Britannicum* (1652).
Berthelot, P. E. M., *Collection des Anciens Alchimistes Grecs* (Paris, 1888).
Goodrick-Clarke, N., *Paracelus – Essential Readings*, (Crucible, 1990).
Maier, M., *Atlanta Fugiens*, trans. & ed. Joscelyn Godwin, (Phanes Press, 1989).
de Rola, Stanislas K., *The Secret Art of Alchemy* (Thames and Hudson, 1973).
Trismosin, *Splendor Solis*, (manuscript of 1682) translated by 'J.K.', (Yogi Publication Society, Illinois).
Waite, A.E. (ed.), *The Hermetic Museum* (1893); first English translation 1768.

Books of interest on alchemy and related subjects:
Ambix (periodical), edited F. Sherwood Taylor, London.
Barbault, Armand, *Gold of a Thousand Mornings* (Spearman, 1975).
Boehme, Jacob, *The Signature of All Things (Signatura Rerum)* (James Clarke, 1969).
Capra, Fritjof, *The Tao of Physics* (Wildwood House, 1975).
Cockren, Archibald, *Alchemy Discovered and Restored* (reprinted by Health

Research, California, 1963).

Dobbs, Betty, *The Foundations of Newton's Alchemy* (CUP, 1975).

Flamel, Nicolas, *Explanation of the Hieroglyphicall Figures* (1624).

French, Peter, *John Dee* (RKP, 1972).

Geber (Jabir), *Works*, ed. E. J. Holmyard (Dent, 1928).

Gilbert, R. A., *The Golden Dawn: Twilight of the Magicians* (Aquarian Press, 1983).

Godwin, Joscelyn, *Robert Fludd* (Thames and Hudson, 1979).

The Hermetic Journal, edited by Adam McLean (quarterly).

Hopkins, A. J., *Alchemy: Child of Greek Philosophy* (AMS Press Inc., 1967).

Jung, C. G., *Memories, Dreams, Reflections* (Collins/RKP, 1963).

——, *Psychology and Alchemy* (RKP, 1953).

Needham, Joseph, *Science and Civilization in China* (CUP, 1956).

——, *The Shorter Science and Civilization in China* (CUP, 1978).

Pauwels, L. and Bergier, F., *The Morning of the Magicians* (Avon Books, 1968).

Paracelsus, *Archidoxes of Magic* (Askin, 1975).

——, *Hermetical and Alchemical Writings*, ed. A. E. Waite (1894).

Powell, Neil, *Alchemy: The Ancient Science* (Aldus Books, 1976).

Scott, Walter (tr.), *Corpus Hermeticum* (Dawsons, 1969).

Sutherland, C. H. V., *Gold* (Thames and Hudson, 1959).

Taylor, A. M., *Imagination and the Growth of Science* (John Murray, 1966).

Thorndike, Lynn, *A History of Magic and Experimental Science* (Columbia University Press, 1923–58).

Vaughan, Henry, *The Complete Poems* (Penguin, 1976).

Vaughan, Thomas, *The Magical Writings*, ed. A. E. Waite (Health Research, California, 1974).

Wilhelm, Richard (tr.), *The Secret of the Golden Flower* (RKP, 1965).

Yates, Frances, *Giordano Bruno and the Hermetic Tradition* (RKP, 1964).

——, *The Rosicrucian Enlightenment* (RKP, 1972).

INDEX

ARCADIA
MUSIC OF THREE CENTURIES 1500–1800

SPLENDOR SOLIS

The Dawning of the Italian Baroque

featuring

Cherry Gilchrist - soprano
Steve Graham - theorbo, baroque guitar
Colin Booth - harpsichord

composers include
Monteverdi, Grandi and Frescobaldi

£5.95

(including UK postage)

tapes available from:

Arcadia, 34 Somerset Street, Kingsdown,
Bristol, BS2 8LY

A digital Arcadia recording from the period
discussed in Chapter 5